FOR SUCH A TIME

The story of the young
Florence Booth

by

Jenty Fairbank

Salvati ... ks
The Salvation Army I ... quarters
London, I

First published 2007

Copyright © 2007
The General of The Salvation Army

ISBN 978-0-85412-759-7

Cover design by Nathan Sigauke

Published by Salvation Books
International Headquarters, The Salvation Army
101 Queen Victoria Street, London EC4P 4EP, United Kingdom

Printed by UK Territory Print & Design Unit

Contents

FOR SUCH A TIME

The story of the young Florence Booth

Acknowledgements

MY years as Archivist/Director of The Salvation Army's International Heritage Centre brought a deep appreciation of the professional skills of my colleague and Senior Researcher, Gordon Taylor. These skills have in no way diminished with his promotion to the post of Archivist, and this book would have been the poorer without the ready aid of Gordon and fellow-researchers Commissioner Karen Thompson and Alex von der Becke.

Jenty Fairbank
Lieut-Colonel

Foreword

ONE of the most striking things about the second generation of Salvation Army leaders was their extreme youth. Florence Soper, a doctor's daughter from Blaina in South Wales, was nine years old when her mother died. She went to live with her aunts in London for her education, and was just 19 when she accompanied the equally youthful Kate Booth to France to begin The Salvation Army in that land. As soon as possible after her 21st birthday, Florence married Kate's brother Bramwell. Their life together was marked by loyalty and love, with strong commitment to the cause of Jesus Christ and to social justice.

As The Salvation Army engages with social justice issues around the world in the 21st century, there is renewed interest in the path trodden by the pioneers. Young people are being inspired by role-models from earlier days. They see the need around them and they want to do something about it.

When Lieut-Colonel Jenty Fairbank was a young student teacher, 18 years of age, she attended the funeral of Florence Booth in Clapton, East London, England. Now, 50 years later, after a lifetime of service that has taken her to Africa and in and out of many schools and colleges in the United Kingdom, Jenty has written about the young Florence, whose example has meant so much to so many women and girls.

It is our fervent hope that the 'good read' offered by this book will be much more than entertainment and interest. It is offered in tribute to those who, like Florence, are touched to the core by the suffering and hopelessness around them, to the extent that, young or old, they will want to do something to carry on the fight. Like Esther, in Bible times, they will feel a call from God in their inmost souls, 'for such a time as this' (Esther 4:14 *New International Version*).

Helen Clifton, Commissioner
World President of Women's Ministries
International Headquarters

ix

x

CHAPTER 1

ALL YOU WANT NOW IS A WIFE

SHE sat in Bow Street Police Court, her four-month-old baby in her arms, her husband in the dock.[1] It was her 24th birthday and her diary entry runs:

Saturday September 12, 1885
Birthday spent in Bow Street Police Court. Quite forgot this a.m. that it was my birthday until, opening letters in cab, found three from home and dear Dad's cheque for £2.0.0. Came out of court 4:30 and thinking pity to wait while B had consultations, came home with Mrs Bulman. Darling one came home with bad blow on nose – been wretchedly mobbed coming out of court by Magistrates door.

'She' was Florence Booth. 'Darling one' was 29-year-old Bramwell Booth, Chief of the Staff to his father, General William Booth, who, with his wife Catherine, had founded The Salvation Army 20 years earlier. In 1878 Catherine had written to her eldest son: 'All you want now is a wife, one with you in soul with whom you could commune and in whom you could find companionship and solace … God will find you one, and I shall help Him … I am praying for one for you.'[2] The result of such a confident liaison with the Almighty was Florence Eleanor Soper.

The eldest of four children of Isbel Soper, a doctor from Devon,[3] England, practising in the mining valleys of Monmouthshire,[4] Florence later wrote: 'The untrammelled existence on the Welsh hills, walking, riding, skating, gave me a love for the simple pleasures of the open air which encouraged me to seek such for

1

our own children.' Yet any vivid recollections she might have had were dimmed by the shock of her mother Jennie's death in 1870, when Florence was only nine years old. More than 60 years later she reflected on this grief in the light of her subsequent experience as a mother and grandmother:

'I think the child's capacity for love, and therefore for sorrow or for joy, is frequently underestimated. I believe that had the depth of my sorrow been understood at that time, and pains taken to probe my feelings, a lasting impression would have been made upon me, and my heart would have opened out more easily then to the influences of religion.

'Children, in relation to the soul and spirit, are less childish than is often thought. How disastrous the consequences of the idea that children must come to "years of discretion" before moral and spiritual questions should be presented to them. Alas, such questions cannot be delayed, one result being that in the secret recesses of the young spirit tiny seeds of doubt are often sown which spring into noxious plants of infidelity, and make what could be a fruitful plain, smiling in the sunshine of God's light, a poisonous morass spreading a miasma of evil gases which suffocate faith and love.'[5]

Elsewhere she describes herself as being 'naturally very lacking in feeling and sentiment – one of the cold, practical natures'.[6] Could the trauma occasioned by her childhood loss explain why?

On her deathbed Jennie Soper had committed the four children to the care of her elder sister. But Florence was far more preoccupied with her father's loss than her own: 'From that hour he became my hero to whom I purposed to devote my life. I quarrelled with destiny because I was born a girl. A boy could be much more his companion, and could become a doctor and share his work. This thought added a spice of bitterness to life for the next ten years.'

At 15 she was sent to a boarding school in Sydenham run by her aunts, the Misses Louie and Emily Levick. During her last term there, in the spring of 1880, her aunts were discussing over the breakfast-table one morning an article in *The Christian* criticising The Salvation Army. Florence's curiosity was aroused when, having read out the verse of a song quoted in the article, her aunt refused to let her read it for herself. Nevertheless, read it she later did, amused by the refrain:

> *The devil and me we can't agree;*
> *I hate him and he hates me!*[5]

Such was her introduction to the Movement which, unbeknown to her at the time, was to command her loyalty for the remaining 77 years of her life. Until then she had long resented any approach made by religious folk hoping to influence her:

'It was my fault, undoubtedly, but those who desired to help me failed to show that religion was a great adventure, which called for sacrifice and courage, for skill and devotion in this life. They gave me chiefly the idea that to become religious meant to receive a gift, a treasure for which I felt that I had no present use or desire.'[4]

Meanwhile, it fell to the Rev Henry Stevens, vicar of Holy Trinity, Sydenham, to prepare Florence and her sister for confirmation. Was he aware that the elder of the two had sat Sunday after Sunday counting the minutes of, what were to her, his long, wearying sermons?

'He failed to help me, I think, because he took too much for granted, not realising that many of us were not moved by religious conviction, but had become candidates for confirmation as a mere matter of form. I had been drifting very far away from any real faith in God. Several months before I had deliberately ceased from prayer by my bedside. I can remember clearly kneeling one evening by a cane chair and looking through at the pattern on the wallpaper behind, and feeling the futility of this, to me, mere form. I could not believe that praying made any difference. I did not realise any true help in the confirmation classes, though Mr Stevens gave us interesting information on Church history and some instruction in doctrine and Bible study; but nothing, so far as I can remember, that was likely to help me to know my true condition. I am sure I was to blame, and probably much was said that would have helped had I been in a different condition of mind and heart towards God.'

Whatever else was lacking in Florence, sincerity certainly was not. During the confirmation service, on being reminded by the bishop of the promises made on her behalf by her godparents that she should 'renounce the devil and all his works, the vain pomp and glory of the world', she realised she had no such intention. She was looking forward to going out into the world and enjoying those vain things to the utmost. Instead of responding to the bishop, she resumed her seat.[5] That day the work of the Holy Spirit in convincing her of sin had begun, preparing her to become his perfect answer to Catherine Booth's 1878 prayer.

CHAPTER 2

THOSE BEAUTIFUL EYES

HER last term at school having concluded, 18-year-old Florence spent the Easter holidays visiting places of interest in London, being permitted for the first time to attend evening entertainments. She was entranced by the theatre, revelling in performances by Henry Irving and Ellen Terry, but it was an evening at the Steinway Hall which was to make the deepest impression on her.[6]

One Sunday[2] her aunts were taking some friends and older pupils to hear Catherine Booth. Florence accompanied them, curious to hear a woman preach:

'Though we were not at the front, her beautiful eyes seemed to look straight into my face, and I felt strangely that she must know all about me.[6] Mrs Booth brought home to me the reality of my position spiritually. In a few moments, as I sat quietly listening, I began to tremble as I realised my desire to avoid God and His claims, and my determination to take my own way in spite of risks to my safety in the next world. Then the Holy Spirit through her earnest words opened up a new prospect. The humanity of Christ became real and His call to the disciples to follow Him in service and in sacrifice for others suddenly became a call to me also.[4] She read a few verses from the first chapter of Acts, and took for her text the eighth verse, "Ye shall be witnesses unto me."

'As I listened to her I realised for the first time that the religious life is one of great endeavour; something to be accomplished for others; not merely a happiness or escape for oneself. The appeal for sacrifice in the giving up of oneself ... the mystery that we were called to the help of God and given the opportunity of assisting in Christ's work for the world was entirely new to me.'[6]

It was the final meeting of the series, and at the close Mrs Booth urged people who had never before done so to testify. From all parts of the hall members of the congregation rose, telling of their love for Christ and their desire to serve him better.[7]

'A most strange urge came upon me.[6] I felt that if I remained silent I should pass under false colours.[7] To my own astonishment[6] I found myself on my feet, saying with much trembling that I had never before understood what serving Christ meant, but that I wished to give myself to Jesus, and would Mrs Booth pray for me.[7] This action was displeasing to my aunts and they immediately rose and left the hall.'

Florence was unusually silent on the way home, feeling an intense desire to be alone. Late though it was, she fought out the spiritual battle on her knees in her room, a feeling of intense horror coming over her at the thought of the way in which she had struggled to get away from God. She realised that to be pardoned for such conduct was a very wonderful thing: 'The sufferings of Jesus became real to me. I knew Him as the Son of God Who loved me and gave Himself for me. I consecrated myself to love Him and bear witness to Him.'

In the early hours of the morning she wrote to her father telling him of the experience and saying that whereas she would love him as dearly as ever, from now on God must come first. 'The letter was placed in the box on the hall table … and two or three times before the country post I took it out, turned it over in my hand, and almost decided not to post it. I can remember the feeling of relief when it had really gone forth on its way.'

Despite bearing the brunt of Dr Soper's reply, which was full of annoyance that Florence had been introduced to The Salvation Army, Aunt Levick shortly afterwards drew her niece's attention to a letter in *The Christian* from the Rev William Booth. The letter explained that in response to the entreaties of friends to introduce The Salvation Army into France, he was setting apart his eldest daughter for this undertaking, and felt 'especially led to desire the help of some lady who has knowledge of the language and the country to accompany her'.

'We talked it over together,' wrote Florence more than 50 years later, 'and I can recall now the thrill which came over me with the thought that perhaps I might be that companion. I wrote at once, giving brief particulars, telling of the impression made on me by hearing Mrs Booth at the Steinway Hall, and that I had consecrated myself to God's service and was seeking His guidance as to the disposal of my life, and that if I could assist Miss Booth in any way I should be willing for the most menial service. A postcard came in reply, asking me to call one morning and see Mrs Booth at 114 Clapton Common.'

Having never been in that neighbourhood before, when Florence found the common she had some difficulty in finding the house because of a 'To Let' notice in the window (noisy dogs next door had so disturbed Mrs Booth that she told the landlord she would leave, and had herself put up the notice – which, apart from confusing young Miss Soper, had the desired result in persuading the landlord to deal with the dogs).

Walking round the common, feeling very nervous about the interview, thinking that all her chances of success would be lost if she were late, and almost making up her mind to return to Sydenham and abandon her quest, Florence finally noticed the figures '114' above the door of the 'To Let' house.[6] As a maid opened the door to her, a tall young man with coal-black hair and beard came out of the house and passed down the steps. Had she not been so preoccupied with her possible lateness she might have recognised a likeness in his eyes[8] to those 'beautiful eyes' which had seemed to look straight into her face so recently at the Steinway Hall. Be that as it may, *he* certainly noticed the visitor who was inquiring for his mother:

'I noticed that the visitor was an attractive girl of about eighteen, and her appearance impressed me,' Bramwell Booth records in his memoirs. 'She was quietly dressed, but I remember still that there were blue cornflowers in her hat, and I confess to the thought that they became her! I passed on my way, but a kind of mental picture was formed, and it reappeared during the day – a quite unusual thing for me. When I returned home at night I was interested enough to make inquiries. I learned her name. She was one of those who had been blessed at meetings my dear mother was then holding in the West End of London, and had been to her to seek spiritual counsel and advice. That was the first glimpse I had of my dear wife.'[9]

Mrs Booth was alone in the front room. As the girl with eyes as blue[10] as the cornflowers in her hat looked into those 'beautiful eyes' she felt that here indeed was one she could love and serve. 'In response to her kindly questionings, all my reserve vanished. I felt able to tell her of desires and longings I had mentioned to no one.'

Aunt Levick held the view that her niece could be a perfectly good Christian without joining The Salvation Army but, slight though her knowledge of the Army was, Florence realised this would be tantamount to being ashamed of her Saviour. Her father's opposition to the idea troubled her deeply. How far would it be right for her to disobey him, she wondered. Catherine Booth helped her to distinguish between matters of principle and those of lesser significance, advising her to yield as far as possible in everything of lesser import but to be unflinching where principle was involved. One sentence was to remain with her and become a guiding light in many a perplexing circumstance: 'Always give God the benefit of the doubt.'[6]

Before Florence returned home to South Wales, her new-found mother-in-the-Lord arranged a meeting with the second Catherine Booth, even then preparing to (in Salvationist terminology) invade France with the gospel. So it was that on a Friday evening in mid-May 1880 'Miss Booth' (as Victorian etiquette demanded Miss Soper call her) and her young companion formed part of the congregation at the weekly holiness meeting at 272 Whitechapel Road, the headquarters at that time of The Salvation Army. As was the pattern, 'Mr Bramwell', the Chief of the Staff, led the meeting, and although the passage of the years left Florence remembering significantly different details from those held in Bramwell's memory, both are worth recording.

In 1933 Florence wrote: 'I still picture the one who became my husband as he led those meetings; standing at the head of a long table covered with a red cloth, to the sides of which people came and knelt when the invitation was given. His coal-black hair and beard, his eyes so like his mother's, his calm manner of speaking, holding in his left hand a small piece of paper, he seemed to me to be a veritable messenger from Heaven, and his message a proclamation of deliverance from sin here below, bewildering and entrancing and yet passing understanding. He had only lately written the verses of which the first is:

> O when shall my soul find her rest,
> My strugglings and wrestlings be o'er?
> My heart, by my Saviour possessed,
> Be fearing and sinning no more?

'They were sung as a solo by Miss Booth. To say that I received illumination in this meeting is a very bare description of the experience that came to me. Away from the meetings and amongst my friends darkness and doubt sometimes seemed to overwhelm me, and I was told that excitement was wrong, that many of the miraculous changes in character of which I heard were delusions, and that so-called saved drunkards and thieves relapsed into their evil ways again. But the change brought about in my own experience was too real to admit of any doubt. I had heard God's voice and had received gifts from Him. The desire for "more" was too real to be explained away.'

The two young women attended the following Friday's holiness meeting, the possibility and definition of a holy life becoming clear to Florence as 'Mr Bramwell' read and commented on the first chapter of 1 Peter. As she heard the words 'for you are kept by the power of God through faith', light was shed on her darkness and she understood that the work was to be God's work; the strength to keep her from sinning was to be God's strength. She had but to be passive in his hands.

She records: 'As the meeting progressed the light on my mind and heart increased. I was among the first to come forward and kneel. Someone spoke to me about dressing to please God' (but God had *created* the blue cornflowers!) 'and I remember saying, "I am willing to dress in red and yellow if God would let me know He wished it." I trusted God to do all He could in me.

'Again I was sensible of a great change. I was naturally self-willed, and had a fiery temper. For six weeks the rebellion I had often felt had been subdued, kept within bounds, but on several occasions I had left the room hastily to get away from the one who had annoyed me. I realised that this fight was won. I felt a submission, pride was subdued, my apprehension of God was *real*.'[8]

Such was Florence's memory, more than 50 years later, of the second and third occasions she had encountered her future husband. He, however, writing in the late 1920s, seems not to have been aware of her having been present in the May meetings. From the glimpse he had of blue cornflowers on the steps of his parents' home in the spring of 1880 Bramwell leaps to the following autumn for his next memory of her:

'It was at a morning Holiness Meeting in our hall near the Whitechapel church. The meeting concluded with the administration of the Lord's Supper, as our custom then was. Florence Soper – for that was her name – had in the interval decided to join The Salvation Army, and she was present that day as one of ourselves. I had not noticed her until I passed round calling upon each one present to remember our Lord's death. This was really the first occasion on which I spoke to her. I have often recalled the circumstance with a momentary but very real pleasure.

'That day I was formally introduced to my future wife by my sister, and we walked some distance together on the way from one meeting to another. Naturally we spoke of the Army and the difficulties for those situated as she was – one of a family then quite hostile to our work. I liked her courage and quick intelligence, but certainly at that time I was not attracted to her in any personal or romantic way.'[9]

Bramwell's reference to her having in the meanwhile decided to join The Salvation Army takes us back to Florence's May willingness 'to dress in red and yellow if God would let me know He wished it'.[8] Discovering that not only were Friday night holiness meetings part of the regular spiritual fare of her new Salvationist friends, but all nights of prayer were too, she attended one in which 'the Founder' (as William Booth became known), Mr Bramwell, Miss Katie and Miss Emma Booth all took part. Testimonies featured, several folk standing at once, so anxious were they to speak. She was somewhat frightened to see others prostrated by violent enthusiasms, and as she watched them being carried out into the lobby she wondered whether she would ever be overcome in a similar way. She concluded that anyone trained in self-restraint as Dr Soper's children had been could not be so overcome. Nevertheless there were to be times in her spiritual pilgrimage when she would receive realisations of the nearness of God and a sense of joy in his love which would bring overflowing tears such as at this time she could never have thought possible.

Leaving the hall at 6 am, she bought from a stall in the lobby a blue ribbon, 'The Salvation Army' marked on it in gold, which, tied round her arm, provoked an occasional jeer from among the crowds of men streaming over London Bridge into the City. A woman also travelling to Sydenham asked what the words on the ribbon meant, not having heard of the Army. Florence found it easy to share her new experience. 'Oh, that I could have your courage!' this fellow-Christian exclaimed.

Florence records: 'From that moment I understood the advantage of The Salvation Army ribbon ... or brooch. Before I went home to Blaina I had begun to wear the brooch, a shield with the same words. In those days they were about two inches square and could be read from afar. This eye-gate witness helped me through the first months at home.'[8]

CHAPTER 3

RATHER LIKE GETTING MARRIED

FLORENCE'S arrival home was what she described as 'a trying experience'. Her father was greatly annoyed at the recent turn of events, and his eldest daughter's resolve – in the light of Mrs Booth's counsel – to keep herself separate from the world resulted in her being very much set in her own opinions:

'It was a great grief to me to be in opposition to my father whom I had always studied to please. I felt I could no longer take a hand at whist. I was rather doubtful about supplying music while card games were going on. The music I felt it my duty at other times to render, for my father had given me the best opportunities for study under Sterndale Bennett and Ebenezer Prout and others. ... Looking back now I can see that I was extreme ...but ... without this I might have made shipwreck.'

Nonetheless she earnestly sought ways to help those around her. Although forbidden to attend Salvation Army meetings, she arranged with the captain of the local corps to leave the side door ajar during the 7 o'clock 'knee-drill' (prayer meeting) on Sunday mornings, so that she could kneel just inside the door (this on chilly early winter mornings). For several Sundays, though not taking part audibly, she felt refreshed by the hour's singing, prayer and Bible reading. A busybody of a patient reported this to the doctor, however, and from then on her only contact with the Army consisted in falling behind the family group making their way to church, and saluting the colours as the Salvationists marched up the high street.

A letter to Bramwell's favourite sister reveals how perplexing life was for the just turned 19-year-old at this time:

'My dear Emma, I am wishing so much today that I could have you here. Life seems to get more and more difficult, it is like a slow breaking of your heart. Papa hardly ever speaks to me now as he used to do and tries as much as possible to make me do what he knows I cannot do happily … Yesterday in the morning when I was writing my tracts to put in the surgery basket, he wanted me to go and practise, and then after lunch I had to go a long walk with a party of friends to go over Ebbw Vale Steel Works, and when we came home Papa insisted on my going to a musical evening, saying he knew I wished to live only to myself and wanted to be shut up altogether, but that I must be sociable for his sake, and so I was obliged to go.

'I am afraid we cannot start our Mothers' meetings. Papa seems so averse to it, so what seemed such a hopeful beginning has proved a failure, or almost one.' (It was to be another 27 years before Florence was able to bring that 'hopeful beginning' to fruition in the launching of an international women's movement – The Home League.)

Once or twice the writer of tracts for the surgery basket was cheered by finding an answering message such as this: 'Dear friend – still keep on this good work, keep believing and God will crown your efforts. – Yours, A Friend.'[8] Busybodies weren't the only ones to visit the surgery evidently! Keep believing Florence did, and the situation was at least partially resolved in due time.

'Perhaps I exaggerated the narrowness of the path, but I have no doubt that this, more than anything else, brought my father to be willing to part with me. The conflict between us as to matters such as card-playing, wearing jewellery and attending social gatherings made the home so unbearable, and his realisation that I should probably influence my sisters and brother brought him to be willing to let me go to France with Miss Booth.'[6]

Nevertheless, Kate Booth's part in persuading the good doctor to change his mind should not be underestimated. Responding to an invitation from Florence to visit Blaina, Kate, with her 'fascinating personality', captured the entire family, not least

Florence's stepmother (her mother's sister, to whose charge she had been specially committed on her mother's death).

On 29 November 1880 Florence wrote a detailed account to her Sydenham aunt of Kate's visit: 'My darling Aunty, How I wish I could tell you everything ... Miss Booth had some long talks with Mama first and she seems to have helped her immensely (if I may say so) ... She seems so much braver about the right and to understand me better.

'The effect about France was magical. Mama now wishes me to go, says it would be an honour. Miss Booth asked Papa on Friday evening. On Saturday she went to Gloucester, returning on Tuesday. Papa was very "glum" while she was away, but on Friday evening (alone with him) she asked for his answer and he said he had no objection, in fact would rather I went with her than anyone else, and he wished me to go abroad some time. He will not say much about the object of my going and is inclined to talk about what we ought to see, but Miss Booth told him all and even mentioned my perhaps taking part in her meetings, so we are sure he knows all.

'For myself, now it is come to the point I find, instead of the eagerly anticipated pleasure, that leaving home, Lilian, Evie, Fred and Papa and you – in fact all I love and all interests – is hard, but I know it is God's will, for I prayed earnestly that He would use Papa and that his answer, *without any pressure*, should be right and so it is done.

'For dear Miss B. it is immensely hard. I cannot think how she bears up – it means giving up England, her home and all, for *someone* must *always* lead in France, you see, if the work stands. I feel as if I had cast in my lot with her. I think it must be rather like getting married and forsaking father and mother for one. It is certainly a *love* match for I do *love* Miss B.

'On Sunday morning Mama and we three went to the hall with her! Papa gave us a willing permission. She gave us a beautiful little address, principally speaking to the members, sharpening them up as to letting their lights shine and being holy. No one

15

knew she was coming, so the hall was not fuller than usual and the volunteers marched to church and so attracted restless boys and children and we had it comfortable and quiet, but Hannah (the cook) went in the evening and everyone expected Miss Booth and it was *crammed*. Poor things, what a disappointment!

'We took Miss Booth up the mountain on Dorritt (the pony). She did enjoy it. We hope to go again this afternoon ...

'My dress for France is to be made by the same person as Miss B's at the Uniform Department, and I am to wear a bonnet! I feel at least four years older – certainly quite twenty. France seems such a responsibility.'

The letter received at Sydenham from Aunt Levick's brother-in-law paints a far different picture, however: 'With reference to Florrie's proposed visit to Paris, I spoke as clearly and definitely as I could to Miss Booth when she was tarrying here. I regret the extreme views which Florrie at present holds. I have not liked to thwart them because I hope they will eventually be modified. I do not admire the Salvation Army or their proceedings and I should distinctly object to F's acting as a S. A. agent.

'The length of time F may remain is of course uncertain. It will depend partly on the expense and also on the advantage accruing to F. while tarrying there ... I had a talk with her last evening and she has written to Miss Booth. She talks of leaving us on Tuesday, but I have told her to write and ascertain when they purpose starting for Paris. Apart from those considerations, on which we should not agree, it seems to me the visit will be an advantageous one to F because every effort will be made to acquire fluency in the language and there will be constant intercourse with residents. If I am satisfied with F.'s reports, and the expenses are not too heavy, I shall not object to her remaining three or four months.'

A few days after Katie's return to London Mrs Booth wrote to Mrs Soper indicating that three or four other young ladies had offered to go with Katie to France, but none with whom she felt so much congeniality as with 'Florry' [sic].

'I presume that Katie would tell you we have a French maid of 24 to go with them, and I am pleased to say that after being with us four months I consider her to be a really simple, unsophisticated girl. Of course every caution will be exercised as to their entertainment and protection; for this we have the interests of some of the leading Christians in Paris. I feel sure you will have no cause to regret letting Florry [sic] go, as my dear child is far beyond her years both in sense and piety.'[12] (Katie was by then 22.)

Christmas in the Soper household was, as always, memorable, strangely echoing a tradition instituted by William Booth with his own family towards the end of the 1860s when he declared, 'I'll never have a Christmas Day like this again!' True to his word, the following Christmas Day had seen the Booths scattered throughout the East End slums distributing 150 plum puddings, many of them cooked in their own kitchen.[13]

After church on Christmas morning 1880, the Sopers as usual distributed Christmas dinners to the doctor's poorest patients, he himself having carved the baron of beef. Christmas puddings of varying size were already boiled and steaming hot, requiring no further cooking. Each family sent someone to collect the dinner and Dr Soper had a kindly word for them all, often inquiring after those who were sick. To gifts of clothing for the children and shawls for the women, Florence this year added a little letter and a text.

The afternoon and evening saw carollers singing their way across the hills, the newest recruit being thrilled to see Salvationists joining them – though she was taken aback that their music was, to say the least, somewhat uncouth compared with the more sophisticated part-singing of some of the choirs.

She left Wales for London on 18 January, expecting the train from Newport to reach Paddington by 6 pm. Heated carriages and dining cars being luxuries of the future, a basket of provisions for the journey and a leaden foot-warmer accompanied her. Not long after leaving Newport she discovered that in the rush of departure the food basket had accidentally been replaced by another, containing nothing edible, and the foot-warmer was leaking so badly the frost on the floor of the compartment quickly turned to sheet ice. The train proceeded more and more slowly, finally stopping completely. Alone, cold and hungry in an uncannily silent world, Florence could only guess what lay beyond the snow-blocked windows. Her eventual rescuer revealed that several trains ahead of them were buried in deep cuttings and there was nothing for it but for the frozen travellers to decamp to a nearby inn, where fires and food had been ordered. The snowdrifts proved a formidable obstacle course for voluminous Victorian skirts and petticoats, but Florence and her fellow travellers at last found themselves gathered round what she described as 'an old-fashioned open fireplace' with tremendous logs of wood:

'The firelight flickered on my Salvation Army shield, and to my astonishment a lady on the other side of the fire sent her husband across to ask if I were going to France with Miss Booth. I was delighted to find that they were friends of Mrs Booth, Mr and Mrs Billups. They took me under their care and when the train steamed into Paddington at 1 o'clock the next day, and other passengers found that there was no food to be had, Mr Billups was entertained in the station-master's room and we consumed the three hard-boiled eggs and bread – all that remained of the station's store.

'I was more starved than ever before, or since, because at the inn I presided at the coffee urn and had just supplied my fellow passengers, and had only tasted my own coffee, when an alarm that the train was going took us all back to the station. The engine driver had been too hopeful; most of the men returned to the inn, but Mr Billups and several ladies remained – we spent five or six hours on the hard seats until ten o'clock, when the down line had been sufficiently cleared.'[12]

A three-horse cab, secured by Mr Billups, took the three weary travellers to St James's Hall, Regent Street,[14] where, despite treacherous weather conditions, Mrs Booth was speaking to a nearly full congregation. That night Kate and her mother stayed in London with Mrs de Noe Walker, while the General, his three sons and Emma returned to Clapton Common, taking Florence with them.

'The snow was quite deep, up to my knees, when we alighted at Stamford Hill Station,' Florence remembered. 'We walked in single file, the Chief of Staff and his brother first trampling the snow for us to follow.

'These experiences nearly spoiled my chance of going to Paris, for a bad attack of quinsy came on. Had not delay in the arrangements occurred I fear I should have been left behind.'[12]

CHAPTER 4

THE FRENCH EXPEDITION

THE cold which took possession of Florence after that winter journey was a trial at the time, but as arrangements for starting Salvation Army work in Paris were delayed, it was probable that, were it not for her sickness, she would have played so great a part in the London meetings that her father would have withdrawn his consent to her going to France at all.

As it was, she was tenderly nursed by Mrs Booth at 114 Clapton Common, being introduced to hydropathic treatment, including a lamp bath. This involved being seated in a wooden box with a hole in the sloping lid, which closed around her neck, leaving her head outside, a lighted spirit lamp under her chair, her feet in hot water. One can safely assume that 'Mr Bramwell' was not afforded a glimpse of her in this state.

'I felt cooked in it,' she wrote, 'and made myself a little too much of a Spartan by enduring silently until I gave the attendant a fright by fainting – the first time such an experience had overtaken me, for I had not before qualified in resemblance to the young women of the Victorian age as described in the books of that time!

'Later I learned to enjoy this bath and other forms of the water treatment. Our seven children grew up without knowing the taste of any kind of physic,' (one wonders whether their physician of a maternal grandfather was aware of this) 'and were all nursed by me through the common ailments of childhood – scarlet fever, measles and whooping cough – with hot or cold mustard bran packs.

'In serious illness I have several times seen hydropathy work a miracle and the life be spared when doctors had given up hope.

Mrs Booth was very enthusiastic in her belief in the treatment of illness by water, externally and internally, and I became her docile follower, surely redeeming the character usually ascribed to a daughter-in-law towards her mother-in-law!

'The General and Mrs Booth felt that the laws of health should be taught to the people, and poor mothers be qualified to treat simple ailments and to recognise the more serious symptoms of disease that need skilled attention. There were no panel doctors in those days and medical attention was expensive for the working people. The General and Mrs Booth stayed several times at Smedley's Hydropathic Establishment at Matlock. A hydro was opened at Grafenburg House, New Barnet, by Mr Metcalf, where several members of the family received treatment. This introduced them to the neighbourhood of Hadley Wood, where they [would decide] to live when Mrs Booth was taken ill, and where the Founder returned after her funeral. ... Arrangements were made at the first training garrison for the teaching and practice of the treatment, and instructions were published in the textbooks for officers, with careful descriptions of the various treatments.'[15]

Of passing interest may be the fact that, as a cadet, Thomas Galt McCallum, my grandfather, was sent by the Founder to be trained in hydropathy by Mr Metcalf, spending 27 years of his officership as the Army's Medical Adviser – based first at the Clapton Training Garrison and then, in a purpose-built hydro, at the William Booth Memorial Training College, Denmark Hill. Neither should it escape our notice that some quarter-of-a-century after General and Mrs Booth stipulated that the laws of health should be taught to the poor – especially mothers – their Soper daughter-in-law ensured that health education was firmly written into the foundations of her newly-established Home League programme.

St John Ervine's observations on the French expedition are worth dipping into here:

'It is true that [William Booth] had been urged by various people to make an attack on France, but these persons, many of whom were not even French, were chiefly parlour Christians, amiably disposed towards general good works, but not themselves able or disposed to undertake any pioneering. They were certain that God would bless Booth if Booth would engage in this difficult work, but the idea that God would bless *them* if they engaged in it seems not to have occurred to them. Their activity went no further than the suggestion that Booth should do something. Booth did. He chose his eldest daughter, Catherine, to be the leader of the raid. ...

'[His] audacity was never more brilliantly displayed than it was on this occasion. The idea of sending an inexperienced girl of twenty-two to evangelise a foreign country in which the prevailing religion was Roman Catholic, and apparently alien in every respect to that which Booth professed, must have seemed to many worldly-wise persons both daft and insensate. The cynical scepticism of the French, too, made such an adventure as Booth now proposed seem absurd. The general British opinion of the French was not flattering, and several excellent ladies and gentlemen went privily to Booth to inquire if he realized what he was doing. They were shocked to find that he was determined to send a young and unprotected female into a country whose inhabitants were notoriously addicted to amorous pursuits!

'The Countess Cairns, a most pious lady, a faithful admirer of the Booths, and a staunch supporter of their work, expostulated with Mrs Booth, who acknowledged that she felt appalled by some "papers I read on the state of Society in Paris" which made her "shudder" and caused her to "see all the dangers to which our darling will be exposed"; but she was sure, and told Lady Cairns so, that the girl's innocence would be her strength. "Katie knows the Lord." ... The fact that British belief about French morals was largely ridiculous does not affect the courage with which Mrs Booth agreed to expose her daughter to what seemed to her dreadful danger.'[16]

What's more, Mrs Booth agreed to expose doctor's daughter Florence Soper and clergyman's daughter Adelaide Cox to the same dreadful danger. When the report that the Booths were sending a group of young women to Paris spread to France it caused commotion among the religious of that land. *The War Cry* of 3 February 1881, page 4, reported: 'From all parts of France we have received letters. Of warning. Of advice. Of entreaty to come. Of entreaty to stop away. Of impatient enquiry, "What are you going to do?" and so on *ad lib.* Thanks to all our friends. Even to the dear, trembling souls who met together to pray the Lord to keep us out of their dear France. Thanks to you all. We only want to do you good, and by God's help we will.'

From the vantage point of 1933 Florence remembered the dedication of the French pioneering party to have taken place in the Strand's Exeter Hall.[15] *The War Cry* report of the occasion appearing two weeks after the event, however, located it in St James's Hall, Piccadilly. Both accounts agree that it took place on Friday 4 February,[17] and, reported *The Christian*, 'the people came forth in their thousands'.[18]

Each member of the packed congregation received a personal appeal from Kate Booth in the form of a leaflet:

'*February 4th.* Dear Friend – I feel the Lord has called me to work for Him in France. Had I chosen a path for myself, I would have very much preferred to stay here in dear old England, where the Lord has given me so much joy, and so much blessing – among my own people, and my own kindred. But having seen how greatly the Army has been used among the uncared-for and lost in this country I long to plant the same standard amid the darkness and misery of beautiful France.

'Friends tell me that the expenses connected with our effort will be very heavy, and this gives me some anxiety. I cannot bear to think of taking money sent for the dear English work, and so I feel I ought to ask in faith for a THOUSAND POUNDS today. Will you help me? I have willingly given the Lord myself for France, and am leaving home and friends to do what I can to bring her people to Jesus – will you share some of the burden with me, and send to me today what you can towards this money which I so much need for the Master's use? Your Sister in Jesus, CATHERINE BOOTH.'

Her father reminded those gathered that it was 12 months almost to the day since a meeting of similar character had been held at Whitechapel to set apart pioneer officers for Salvation Army work in the United States of America, and only a matter of weeks since another meeting had set apart officers for Australia.

Ever aware of the need to publicise the Army's work if purse strings were to be loosened, the General then took opportunity to use the occasion to chart progress over the past three years:

'In May 1877 we had twenty-nine stations; in Christmas 1880, 172 stations. In 1877 we employed thirty-one Officers; last Christmas, including those in training, we employed 363 Officers, exclusive of those in America. We had in May 1878 fifty-five Theatres and Concert Halls employed; we have now 224. In May 1877 we had 625 voluntary speakers; we have now (exclusive of America) 6,180. In 1877 we held 16,000 services; last year we held 166,000. In 1877 our poor people raised £4,200; in the last year they raised and spent themselves, without coming on to our books at Headquarters, but under our oversight and direction, £17,669.

'We commenced *The War Cry* twelve months ago with a circulation of 20,000, and, after wavering for a few weeks it steadied and increased until our circulation reached 120,000. We hope to make it a quarter-of-a-million before this year closes. We have now a *War Cry* in America, and we expect we shall have a *War Cry* before many weeks have gone by in France, and by the blessing of God we will have a *War Cry* in every nation under the sun, for in every one of them we propose to raise a cry of war. We propose to dispute the Devil's right to hold and to occupy a single foot of this redeemed world.'

Mr T. A. Denny and his brother Edward had each agreed to give a hundred pounds to the French expedition if a thousand pound were raised that day. Five hundred pounds was immediately forthcoming from the congregation.[17] Forthcoming from 'the Army Mother' (as Mrs Booth was affectionately becoming known) was a Salvation Army flag, handmade by her.[19]

'We are told by an eye-witness,' empathised her eldest granddaughter almost 90 years after the event, 'that … she was observed to be deeply agitated. …

'In those days "foreign" still had a menacing sound to the ordinary person. Travelling, except for the rich, was a much more isolating experience than it is today. The bloody scenes of the Paris Communes were barely ten years away, and French ferocity and lawlessness got exaggerated in the atmosphere that hung over France like dust from the explosion of the first revolution eighty years before. Catherine certainly believed that a great part of French society was monstrously wicked.'[20]

Yet, once addressing the enthralled congregation, she gained courage, declaring:

'All our confidence is in the Holy Spirit. We should not be so foolish as to send so frail an instrumentality if we believed it depended on human might or strength, but we do so because we know that it depends on divine strength and because we believe that our dear child is thoroughly and fully given up to God, and is casting herself upon Him for strength, holding fast to the divine promise that He will be her sufficiency for this work.'

The meeting's climax came as Katie stepped forward with her two predictably nervous young companions to receive the Army colours – emblematic of the Trinity – her mother giving them the following charge: 'My dear child and my dear young friends – I consider it an honour, in the name of our Divine Commander-in-Chief, and in the name of the General of this Army, to present you with this flag, as an emblem of the office and position you sustain, and I pray that He may give you grace to uphold the truths which this banner represents, and establish on a permanent and solid basis The Salvation Army in France. Oh, that He may give you grace to carry it into the slums and alleys, wherever there are lost and perishing souls, and to preach under its shadow the everlasting Gospel of the Lord Jesus Christ, so that through your instrumentality thousands may be won from darkness, infidelity, and vice, to Him their Lord and their God.'

Towards the end of her response to this charge Katie gives a hint that the recent hydropathic treatment undergone by Florence might not have been totally effective: 'I am taking with me a dear friend who has left all for Jesus, and who would speak, but her sore throat will not allow her. She is of one spirit with myself, and has only one desire, and that is to give her all for Jesus. And another girl I am taking, too, who has been converted, and who I believe will stand by The Army, and stand by the colours, and fight for King Jesus.'[17]

Assuming that the 'other girl' was Adelaide Cox, one cannot help but remark on the contrast in Kate's way of referring to her, after having called the sore-throated one 'a dear friend'. It is to be hoped that Adelaide's clergyman father was not present! Wrote Florence in her diary: 'What a great step I took today! I can never go back now, never accept any lower life. All I have to do is to trust in God to make my way clear. I pray for Papa that he may come to see what a great privilege it is for me. The thought of the responsibility seems overwhelming, but the Lord's strength will be made perfect in my weakness.'[15]

Four further farewell meetings were called at short notice within the next few days – at Whitechapel, Sheffield, Nottingham and Newcastle upon Tyne – resulting in a further £70 or so for France. There is no mention of Florence and Adelaide being present. At Nottingham 'Mrs Ridsdel, the wife of the major, gave her child away to the Lord for France, promising to train it for this purpose, and when ready to send it over to Miss Booth, who the next morning at the train accepted, kissed, and blessed the offering.'[18] Did France ever hear anything more of 'it', one wonders?

Not until the end of February, therefore, did the little group leave for Paris, but Florence, having bidden farewell to her family in mid-January, did not return home meanwhile. It might be assumed from her account of her father's opposition both to her conversion and to her association with The Salvation Army that he was a man of little or no religious sensibility. Yet his farewell letter as she left for France was tenderly expressed, bringing her much comfort:

'February 27th 1881 – A fall of snow delayed the post this morning and it was verging on 2 p.m. when the letters arrived. We were surprised to learn that you were starting tomorrow. You cannot realise, darling, the longing anxiety we feel, and how anxiously we shall long for tidings. It is well that you should not, and it would not do for the young to realise at twenty years the experience of fifty years. Still our source of strength is the same, and as Jacob prayed that "the angel which redeemed him from all evil might bless and preserve" the sons of Joseph, so shall we pray, beloved one, that our God may supply your every need, and bless you in your going out and coming in, preserving you in every danger, and bringing you home to us in peace and safety. ... Do not let your zeal get the better of your judgement. You know it is not always in accordance with our own wish that we can expect God's blessings. Use every means to fit yourself for the discharge of any duty, and be assured that it is your part to learn now that you may teach hereafter. God bless you and your companions on your journey.'[15]

Crossing the Channel on a small paddleboat was a great adventure for the girl who had never been farther than a summer trip round the Eddystone lighthouse. Unwittingly she and 'Miss Cox' strayed out of bounds, climbing into the prow to sit on a coil of rope – only to be angrily turned out as they approached harbour, the rope being vital for tying-up purposes.

Their initial silence as the separation from home and friends began to take effect gradually gave way to a sharing of confidences and the discovery that although (perhaps because) Adelaide Cox's father was a clergyman, she had experienced much the same kind of difficulty in obtaining parental consent as had Florence. The fact that she felt the same clear conviction of God's way for her being the way of The Salvation Army, and that she too had been helped by Mrs Booth's West End meetings, meant that the two were greatly drawn to one another in those first days in a strange land. It was a friendship which was to prove mutually helpful through very many years.[15]

CHAPTER 5

THE SANDWICH-BOARD CARRIER

'MR BRAMWELL' had been present at the pioneering party's farewell meeting in St James's Hall, and shortly before his death, 48 years later, he recorded having heard the 'few words' Florence said from the platform on that occasion.[21] In the light of Katie's reference to the sore throat, we may suppose that either what Salvationists used to refer to as the exigencies of the war had called him from the platform during the gathering, or that his always problematic deafness[22] prevented him from hearing whether she had actually spoken a few words or not. Either way, he later recorded what he presumed had happened.

He is, however, quite clear that:

'... by one of those curious "accidents" which can never be entirely explained, I had the opportunity of rather a lengthy conversation. I could not say that I was then in love, but I certainly found myself at the end of our talk in deep *sympathy* with a striking and attractive young woman, one who was now an officer with us, who had suffered considerable loss and hardship for her Lord and His cause, and who seemed completely consecrated to the service of the Lord Jesus Christ, as I understood that service.

'A day or two after this the French party left us, and I found myself reflecting on the impression made upon me. I sought to know also the impression made on my mother and on my sister Emma, the Consul, and learned that it was quite good. Altogether, I began to feel myself drawn to the now absent captain.

'Then straightway I fell into a serious controversy. Grave questions presented themselves. I saw little prospect of being able

29

to provide a home suited to receive one of whose home life I had already learned something, and one who, I saw for myself, must have been all her life sheltered and delicately cared for and, no doubt, accustomed to much that I should hardly dare approve. I shrank also from the possibility of being hindered in my work for God and the souls of men by allowing another absorbing interest to come into my life. Was it wise – safe? Was it right? I felt myself irrevocably covenanted with God for that work, and I dreaded putting myself into circumstances which might make me less fully devoted to it.

'I realized also that the rush and care of that life, as it already seemed likely to develop, could scarcely be favourable to guiding and training one whose experience of spiritual things had been but brief, and that I ought to bear in mind that her soul was as precious as my own. I halted.

'Still, I found that I had undoubtedly come under a new influence, and the question arose, "Might not this be God's way for me?" I decided to give myself six months for deliberation and prayer before coming to a decision or taking any step whatever in the matter. I did so. Again and again during that time I concluded that I should be wise to give up all thought of the subject, but again and again I came back to its consideration.'[21]

Meanwhile the 'new influence', totally oblivious of the deep impression she had made on the General's son, was coming to terms with impressions of a wholly different kind.

'My first impression of Paris', she wrote, 'was painful ... Our hall was situated in one of the poorest quarters near the Place de la Republique and Boulevards Voltaire and St Denis ... and the difficulty of women appearing in public had not been sufficiently understood.

'The meetings were made known by placards. Miss Cox and I acted as sandwich-board carriers, and marched in the gutter up and down the streets in the neighbourhood, followed soon by a curious crowd. So far as gathering a congregation this was a success, and perhaps also from the Salvation Army point of view,

30

as the very worst characters of the neighbourhood were assembled. The police soon forbade this method of advertisement. ...

'The entire absence of any foundation of moral or religious thought to appeal to was a shock to me. ... Men worked long hours. Before six in the morning the trains brought thousands of them in their blue smocks into the city, on Sundays as well as weekdays. [We] sallied forth with bundles of the French *War Cry*, entitled *En Avant* [Forward!], as the words "War Cry" were forbidden by the French authorities.

'We cannot forget our experience as we stood on the corners of streets selling as fast as we could. Morning after morning this went on, until the eagerness to buy relaxed, and we received jeers and taunts instead. It is well, I am sure, that we had not the least idea of the thoughts of those men who at first were so eager to buy. Undoubtedly they looked upon us as abandoned women.'[15]

Undoubtedly they did, and undoubtedly those same men, given the chance, would have done far more than simply 'look upon' these strange young English women had Katie's suggestion for the name of the paper been allowed to prevail. Her schoolgirl French saw no reason why it should not be called *Amour*. Neither could she initially understand her lieutenants' objections to parading the streets of Paris crying '*Amour*, un sou!'[23]

In a report for English friends *la Maréchale* (as Bramwell dubbed Katie[24]) wrote: 'At the first, our audiences were anything but attentive. Our hall in the Rue d'Angouleme, standing in a court approached by a narrow street, was filled mainly with people who had no idea of worship or of good manners. Every mispronunciation of a French word, every unexpected gesture or unusual circumstance, would cause a roar of laughter; and when any of the audience interrupted us specially, the rest would rise to their feet and there would be a hubbub for a few moments. If one specially troublesome person was singled out for removal from the hall by the police, many others would leave with him, and as there were generally a gathering of roughs in the court, there would be a disturbance there until the police cleared it entirely. Imagine our

31

carrying on services of this kind for about a fortnight before we saw one real penitent!'[25]

A French Christian who watched these first struggles advised Katie, 'You had better go home to your mother. The Salvation Army cannot possibly succeed here; your efforts will be utterly useless.' But *la Maréchale* was made of sterner stuff. 'If I cannot save France I can die for it,' she replied.[26]

Other Christian friends who came to help, rather than discourage, nevertheless did not share the seemingly inexhaustible patience of the *Salutistes*. One, who found fault with the disturbers, was followed by the mob after leaving the hall, and had his head pushed through a shop window. A complaint was made to the police, who ordered the hall to be closed. Wrote Florence to Aunt Levick:

'We have so much anxiety at present. The Préfet of Police has stopped the meetings. We hardly know what course to take and are waiting advice from London. If we have any meeting tonight we shall be *arrested*. We are still believing, and I am sure God has not brought us here for nought – all this furniture bought, house taken, hall leased – and above all the real good done. I never was in such circumstances and I have never felt God so near, or felt so much that I am ready for anything, death if necessary, for Him and His work.

'I feel the utmost contempt for the government officials of every sort that it is possible to have. To the Commissioner of Police that came here this morning my teeth actually gnashed of their own accord at him. I could not help their grating together.'[22]

The Préfet visited the hall while elsewhere Katie was pleading with the Commissioner of Police to give them protection and allow meetings to continue. But the return of the Préfet decided the matter. As he lay down his pistol he remarked: 'I was never so frightened in all my life. You had got half the cut-throats of Paris there.' The decree was made and the hall was closed.

It seemed a long six weeks before 'London', in the diminutive shape of Mrs Booth, was able to bring about the resumption of meetings. This she did by persuading the Lord Mayor of London, the City Chamberlain, the Commissioner of the Metropolitan Police and Lord Cairns[22] to sign a guarantee of the Army's 'reputableness'.[27] Lamented Florence: 'We were very sorry to find that we never afterwards gathered congregations so much to our liking, for the idea of being under police suspicion made many of the men afraid to attend.'[25]

By June she had already been away from home much longer than her father had originally intended. All his letters spoke of her returning home for good, yet she increasingly felt that she could only be happy with 'Miss Booth' and as a soldier of The Salvation Army:

'A spiritual battle was fought out on my knees, for I realised that God's Will must be first, even before what we think to be God's work. The sentence in my father's farewell letter helped me. "You know it is not always in accordance with our own wish that we can expect God's blessing."'

And there, amidst all the turmoil, slipped into her diary on 18 June – almost as an afterthought – are the words: 'The Chief of Staff came to see his sister and has cheered us up so much. He spoke about my arrangements and thinks the Lord will open my way.' On 28 July she wrote: 'Crossed over from France. Oh shall I ever go back? Thy will be done.'[25]

After a few days in Cromer with 'Miss Booth', Florence spent Sunday 7 August in London with the Booths, attending the morning meeting at Whitechapel, led by 'Mr Bramwell'. The next day, wearing her navy blue uniform dress and bonnet, she went home to Blaina, feeling it right to show outwardly what in her heart she really was. In consequence Dr Soper was all the more obdurate that she should not return to Paris. Her diary entry for 1 September reads:

'I am learning to say "Thy will be done." This is the Cross He asks me to take up – to leave all my hopes and ambitions of serving Him in France and of leading some of those dear, dark souls to His feet, but above all to cease helping her, to let her go into that dark battle when I might have been by her side. I know her better than any other there. I must stay here and fight against odds only known to myself, with my heart-strings drawn asunder, for I love Papa, too, and yet now our ways are apart – but I have forsaken all for Jesus and will wait His Word to go again to the front.'

As it happened, she did not have long to wait for that 'Word'. It came, as it had done a year earlier, in the form of Kate Booth, who, on Florence's birthday, paid a surprise visit to the Sopers. She stayed three days. 'She has gone,' records the diary for Wednesday 14 September, 'and the poor, dear father has given his consent until Christmas. God will reward him and make up for my absence.'[25]

Back in Paris, the autumn of 1881 found her more deeply engrossed than ever in Salvation Army work. Katie's sister-in-law, Maud Ballington Booth, later incorporated an account of those early struggles into her book *Beneath Two Flags*:

'It seemed as though the first convert would never come. The people wept, and were evidently impressed, but as to definitely seeking salvation, it seemed far from them. But one night the Captain [*la Maréchale*] made her way to the back of the hall and sat down by a poor, dissolute working-woman; she put her arms around her and asked her if she did not want Jesus as her friend and Saviour. "I love you," she said, looking into the woman's face, while her tears fell on the hard-worked hand. Those tears melted the heart which no amount of preaching would have broken; and this touch of Divine love made the poor woman long to find its Source. So before the night had passed the Army's first Parisian convert had risen from the penitent-form washed in the precious blood of Jesus. The ice was broken then, and though the fight was still hard, by ones and twos their ranks were augmented, until a nice little platform full of saved French men and women could be seen nightly in the new hall on the Quai Valmy.'[28]

The Quai Valmy hall was much larger, holding some 1,200 people, and one can imagine the trepidation with which Florence approached speaking in it. She was so conscious of her inadequacy in the French language that she was often tied to her notes. Yet she must have done better than she herself realised, for in a letter to her mother Katie wrote: 'Florrie spoke wonderfully last night; she has a peculiar style and power of her own. She jumped up and saved us last night. I was about driven to my last extremity. All were astonished. God helped her in a marvellous way and she held the crowd of roughs spellbound.'[25]

The *Salutistes* had been generously supplied with New Testaments to give away, and these were soon much in demand by the young men. Florence's initial joy at this was all too soon dampened by the discovery that the pages were being used as cigarette papers.

'Miss Booth decided we would make a small charge, and though the sale was slow we were satisfied that some were read. A middle-aged man who had attended the meetings for six or seven weeks bought one of the Testaments. "I had a book like this when I was sixteen," he said, "but the priest told me to burn it as I could not understand it, and because I did not do so he took it away from me."

'With great interest we watched him, reading in the dinner hour under the trees on the boulevard. He soon came forward to pray and seek pardon and peace. His wife followed a few days later saying, "I cannot tell you the change in my husband. He is as different now as water from wine. Before he swore terribly, now he does not say a cross word – we are so happy. Peace has come to our house."'[15]

Peace, however, was slow in coming to at least one resident of the house at 114 Clapton Common. Near the end of the six months he had given himself for deliberation and prayer on the matter of the 'new influence' that had come into his life, Bramwell Booth confessed to being very little clearer in his judgment, even though his feelings were stronger – no doubt helped along by that 18 June visit to Paris 'to see his sister':

'I decided to consult the Founder and to accept his view as probably the right one. I told him the exact situation. He asked me if the captain [Florence Soper] knew anything of the matter.

I answered, "No, she could not do so." Then he helped me to test my own feelings, and spoke strong, wise words of counsel and warning. We had prayer, and he finished our interview by approving of my desire, and remarking in his direct if whimsical fashion, that the question now was, "Will she have you?" While half preparing me for a refusal, he gave me his blessing in either event!

'The time now came to put the matter to the test. I went over one evening to Paris, and next morning found Miss Soper with my sister in their apartment in Rue Parmentier.'[29]

CHAPTER 6

BE THE LORD'S AND BE MERRY ABOUT IT!

THE approach to Christmas 1881 cast long shadows on Florence's path, for her father's permission to remain in France would only extend until then. She felt painful doubt as to the course she ought to take, but at the same time a growing conviction that when she became her own mistress she should return to the work she loved.

'All this perplexity was removed as by a miracle,' she subsequently wrote, 'when Mr Bramwell Booth arrived from London early one morning, and after breakfast with us, asked to see me alone. He has written something of what passed between us, but of the astonishment that came upon me he could not write for he did not know, neither had he the least idea of the veneration in which I held him. ... A new conception of life and love was revealed, I understood as in a flash something of what he felt for me, and as my heart responded I became another being.'[30]

More than 50 years later, their eldest daughter revealed that Bramwell then gave Florence 'all the reasons why she should not marry him!'[31] As Bramwell recalled that conversation:

'After breakfast I asked for a few minutes' conversation, and then in the simplest way I could devise I plainly stated my feelings, carefully described something of my experiences during the previous six months, and asked her to be my wife. I felt bound to dwell rather fully on the probable hardships and uncertainties of my future, including the simple style of living I should have to adopt. At the same time I referred to the strain of our fight with a world in arms against Jesus Christ, and the little we could expect in the way of human sympathy or gratitude in the battle against sorrow and sin.

'The captain remained very silent during what had become quite a recital. She was seated at the table. I had risen, and was walking to and fro as I spoke, stirred both by my theme and by my anxiety to be perfectly frank. At last I stopped in my perambulations and said: "Would it be possible, now that you know my feelings, to give me some word as to *your* feelings or probable feelings on the question?"

'"Do you mean *now*?" she asked.

'"Yes," I said, "if possible."

'"How long," was the reply, "did you say you have been praying and considering the matter?"

'"Six months."

'"Well," with a little smile, "perhaps I might ask for six months also?"

'I said, "Certainly!" Of course I could say no other! Then I spoke further – particularly of the possibility of our being of service to one another in working for the blessing and helping of the people. We both desired to see God glorified before anything else. She could help me in this. I would strive to help her.

'I was standing on one side of the room when, at this point, she rose and came near to me and said, "Did I understand you to say that you believed I could *help* you – that I could really be of service to you in your work?"

'I said that that was my sure feeling. I added something about my sense of the seriousness of a proposal to bring her to share in so burdensome and difficult a task as mine. I spoke also of my unworthiness of such a helper. Only the deepest affection, I said, could make it right for either of us to think of it. Then there fell a time of silence between us as we stood together, and I knew that in large part my battle was won.

'We had, however, to consider the views of Dr Soper, and I did not then ask for any formal promises except such as might be given subject to his consent. But we came to a happy conclusion and together committed ourselves to God in prayer, and I humbly felt, as I have felt ever since, how entirely the Lord our God had guided us. I returned to London the same night. It was November 22nd 1881.'[32]

To their daughter, the third Catherine Booth, preparing her father's biography in the early 1930s, Florence confided:

'I had never looked upon Mr Bramwell Booth as an ordinary mortal, which indeed he was not. Such an idea as his ever wanting to marry had never occurred to me, and no word or look from him had ever suggested to me anything of the kind in connection with me.

'The evening before the day on which he spoke to me, his sister talked to me about him in a way I did not at all understand. I must, I think, have been very dense. She hinted at some course she hoped I would take that would be a great pleasure to her. When he made the revelation that he had chosen me after a time of careful consideration, I had the greatest surprise of my life. I had never been able to understand how he could have known enough of me to make it other than a leap in the dark.

'I listened to him without making any remark. I remember my heart began to beat violently and I was conscious that my view of him radically changed. He had always seemed to me to be on a platform of holiness and service infinitely above me, like some angelic being, but in those few moments he became human, a man who had suffered, who was lonely, and I felt that if I could but help him, I knew I could die for him there and then.

'When at last I was compelled to speak I rose and went close to him and while speaking took hold of a button of his coat, which button I found wrapped in white paper in his breast pocket some months after we were married.'

Summed up the third Catherine Booth, who, of all people, knew them both best:

'She was by nature undemonstrative, he under great restraint from a desire to let her well weigh what he regarded as the disadvantages; they nevertheless looked deep into each other's hearts on that November morning in Paris, and were satisfied with what they saw there. No definite answer was asked then, and none was given. It was understood that her father must be approached.'[33]

A difficult time followed for the couple, but not for one moment did Florence question her right to yield her heart to Bramwell, and, when she came of age in 10 months' time, to give herself to him in marriage. Her Grandfather Levick had caused her mother great sorrow by refusing his consent when young Dr Soper asked for her hand. Jennie submitted to her father, but suffered greatly as a result, and when the old man finally relented after many months, her health had been undermined to such an extent that within 11 years she was dead.[30]

On Wednesday 30 November, having announced himself by telegram, Bramwell arrived at Blaina by the evening train. Though his mind was far from wishing to concentrate on the social niceties etiquette required for the first few hours, he finally felt able to request a few moments with the Doctor privately. What transpired is recorded in the letter to Florence he wrote the next day, simply headed 'In the train to London':

'I said plainly to him that I loved you, that for twelve months I have thought about it, and prayed that I might know God's will and do it, and that for six months or more it has steadily grown upon me that God has given our hearts to each other's keeping – that I had let you know when in Paris last week that I felt all this, and that while I had not asked you or wanted you to make me any promise or in any way to express your wish in the matter, yet I had reason from what passed to think that your heart reciprocated something of my wish – and that now I was come on the very first chance that I had, to tell him about it, and ask him to let me take you for my own with his cordial and fatherly approval, if you were willing that this should be so. ...

'I could see the Doctor was very much surprised. ... He said, in substance, that he was perfectly astonished, that he had never contemplated the possibility of such a thing and that he did not know what to say. Then he asked me some questions about money matters, seemed to think that I thought you had some money in your own right – which I did *not* – and we sat silent, as I saw he was feeling a good deal. The Doctor said he would go and speak to Mrs Soper, who had been left in the drawing room. Mrs Soper seemed more surprised than the Doctor, and at first cross-examined me a little, coming round at last very much to my side, as I thought, and finished by saying, "Florrie must settle it." ...

'He said he was not married till 28; I thought perhaps he would have been happier married sooner, and not getting an answer I concluded he thinks so also.'[34] (It is unlikely that Bramwell would have known at this stage of Grandfather Levick's prohibitive stance over Dr Soper's own proposal to Jennie.)

There was much more in this vein, Bramwell summing it all up for Florence with: 'I do not think he is afraid to *trust me* with his treasure, but he is afraid that you are lost in this Salvation maze, and he does not like or trust *that*.'[35]

While awaiting Florence's response to the train letter – in which he had finally asked if she would be his, apparently forgetful of the six months she had requested to pray about the matter – he wrote to the first Catherine Booth: 'Dearest Mother, I feel quite that this matter is all the Lord's arranging ... I am very glad my choice *is* yours, it is and will be an additional happiness difficult to estimate ...'[35]

By this time Florence was replying: 'I am very glad you went, and more glad about the result – I expected something very different. I know this must be from the Lord and the only trouble of my heart is that I feel utterly unworthy of you and unfit for the position in the work. I should be happier if I felt you knew me better – my faults and my shortcomings – as to the rest, such as I am – I am yours. ... I am coming on Thursday. It feels like running from my post sooner than I ought, but I want to see you, and to learn to know you better. Ever your own. I suppose I shall have a letter from papa tonight.'[30]

And so she did. Bramwell in his happiness had not realised that the doctor's comparative silence was caused by amazement. The postscript of her father's reply to his 'beloved Florrie' renders it unnecessary for us to read the body of that letter. He simply wrote: 'P.S. – I wish you distinctly to understand there must be no pledge or engagement entered into.'

Calling at Sydenham on her way home to Wales she found her aunts 'fully informed and awfully savage'. She discovered also that her father had written to them as though utterly heartbroken about it – indeed, they were of the opinion that he would not be able to continue living in Blaina after it was known, and that Florrie would therefore be responsible for breaking up the home. She returned to Paris 'in the dumps' because of the disapproval of those dear to her, Bramwell attempting to cheer her with '... so be the Lord's and be merry about it ...'.[36]

'You say you were as much surprised by the proposition as I was,' was one tactic tried by Dr Soper. 'Accepting this, darling, as really the case, I can only say that you seem to have acted in such a solemn and important decision as this involves, with the same impetuous and impulsive spirit which has marked previous decisions of yours. I am disappointed in my darling girl, who as I trusted would as she grew older allow calm and dispassionate judgment to exercise more sway. Is it possible, darling, that at the very first proposal of the kind, without any preparation you are prepared at once to assent? I am not aware that you had seen much of Mr B. and I should certainly have objected to your being thrown together. ... You have surprised me at your decisions before, but these were trivial compared with the momentous issues involved in this.'

She regretted that she had neglected to tell her father of other occasions when offers of marriage had been met with a decided 'No!' Had she done so, he might have judged her less harshly now.[30]

At the beginning of February 1882 Bramwell's mother waded into the breach with all the sanctified logic her pen could

42

command. As a result, Dr Soper gave reluctant consent to the engagement, anger and active opposition to his daughter's Salvationism now giving place to a settled displeasure and sadness almost harder for her to bear. Furthermore, nursing hopes that it might yet come to nothing, he did not wish the engagement to be made known.[37] In the 47 weeks before their marriage, they were to spend only three or four long weekends together – mostly at the country cottage of, and chaperoned by, Mr and Mrs Billups (friends of the snowstorm) at Barry, near Cardiff.

Starting as he meant to go on, Bramwell's first gift to his love was a copy of Canon Liddon's *Bampton* Lectures.[38]

44

CHAPTER 7

THREE LOUD WHISTLES FROM THE LEADER OF THE BAND

'MR BRAMWELL BOOTH,
CHIEF OF STAFF,
WILL BE MARRIED
AT CLAPTON,
ON THURSDAY,
the 12th OCTOBER,
at Eleven a.m.
BY THE GENERAL'

... announced *The War Cry* of 27 September 1882. Readers were left in the dark as to who the bride might be, even the gilt-printed wedding songbook being simply entitled *Salvation Wedding Songs. To be sung on the occasion of the Marriage of the Chief of the Staff.* On the morning of 12 October the bride and groom – who wore Army uniform throughout the day – were legally married at Clapton register office, having left 114 Clapton Common in a four-wheeled cab, accompanied by Bramwell's brother Herbert and George Scott Railton, the Army's first commissioner, who acted as witnesses. Dr and Mrs Soper, with Florence's brother and two sisters, travelled from Sydenham.[38] What the Sopers made of the day's proceedings can only be imagined.

For one halfpenny, the 19 October edition of *The War Cry* treated its readers to a detailed account of the nuptials, much of it consisting of direct quotes from the *Daily Chronicle*, *Evening Standard* and *Daily Telegraph*:

'Weddings are common-place enough events, but the one which took place yesterday at the Salvation Army Congress Hall, Lower Clapton, possessed features of more than usual interest. All the accessories for which the Salvation Army are famed – the officers in their uniform, from the General and Mrs Booth and family down to the youngest cadet, the brass band of men, and the tambourines of "the Hallelujah Lasses" – lent their aid yesterday to celebrate with becoming distinction, in the midst of an immense audience, the marriage of William Bramwell Booth, "the Chief of the Staff" of the Army, and a son of its founder, to the lady of his choice, Miss Florence Eleanor Soper, a daughter of Dr Soper, of Blaina, in Monmouthshire.

'There are many ways … of raising money, and perhaps to General Booth is due the initiative in showing that even a marriage can be made profitable to the cause of religion, which he upholds so stoutly. Excepting officers and leaders, nearly 6,000 persons who filled the Congress Hall at Clapton yesterday on the occasion of the marriage celebration, paid for admission, and that at the rate of a shilling a head. … Let it, however, be at once stated that the funds so raised, together with the offertory and the presents made to the newly-married couple are destined to help in the liquidation of the balance of £8,000 that still remains unsettled in connection with the purchase for Salvation purposes of the Grecian Theatre and Eagle Tavern, in the City Road' (of 'Pop goes the Weasel' fame).

'Dull though the morning was overhead, and damp underfoot, with rain pouring down, crowds of persons, nearly all of the gentler sex, for women always preponderate at a marriage, found the way down the muddy, unpaved *cul-de-sac* which terminates in the portals of the great building proclaimed in large letters outside to be the "Salvation Army Congress Hall". … Such as had not come provided with tickets, the requisite passports for admission were on sale at the door by men looking not unlike the watermen who bear the banners in the Lord Mayor's show, as they wore red jerseys, having, however, the words "Salvation Army" in letters of gold upon the breast.'

At this point the *Evening Standard* reporter takes over from his *Daily Chronicle* counterpart:

'Shortly after eleven the band went out to meet the bride and bridegroom with their friends, and marched into the building at their head playing. The former were received with cheering and the waving of some thousands of handkerchiefs, whilst loud cries of "Amen" came from all directions. Silence having been demanded by three loud whistles from the leader of the band, the "General" called upon the audience to sing the second hymn. ... Commenting on the words sung, at the end of each verse: "Oh, I am glad there is cleansing in the blood," he expressed his ability to be glad at everything, though most of the newspapers were caricaturing him. Many poor men, he said, were getting a living by blackening the "General's" character, though there was a more profitable and honourable way of making a living and even of making newspapers sell. ... Many persons had written letters sympathising with him, and saying he had a deal to do; so he had, and he enjoyed it; a deal to suffer, so he had, and he enjoyed it. Others said they would not like to be caricatured as he was. He did; he enjoyed it, for those who did it were advertising him for nothing, and they were sure to get someone saved for the caricature.'

The *Daily Telegraph* account is next utilised, its reporter having taken down the General's introductory remarks verbatim:

'The GENERAL: This service is after somewhat an unusual fashion, and may just need one word of explanation, although I have taken up so much time by explanations thus far ... and yet, possibly, this one remark will make everything plain – namely, that The Salvation Army endeavours to act literally upon the direction of the Holy Ghost given by the Apostle Paul – that whatsoever we do, whether we eat or drink, or whatever we do, we should do all to the glory of God. ... The Salvation Army, in whatever it does in this fashion, seeks to promote the glory of the Lord; that whether we have a pleasure seeking meeting, whether we have a festival meeting, a funeral or a wedding, we strive to turn everything to account by making it to promote the glory of God.'

During the marriage ceremony The Salvation Army's articles of marriage were used for the first time[39] and it is worth pausing in our romp through the lengthy proceedings to consider just what the couple were agreeing to:

1. *We solemnly declare that we do not seek this marriage simply to please ourselves, but that we believe it will enable us to better serve and please God, and serve the interests of The Salvation Army.*

2. *We promise never to allow our marriage to lessen in any way our devotion to God or The Army.*

3. *We each severally promise that we will never try to prevent each other from doing or giving anything that is in our power to do or give to help The Army.*

4. *We each severally promise to use all our influence with each other to promote constant and entire self-sacrifice for the Salvation of the world.*

5. *We promise always to regard and arrange our home in every way as a Salvation Army Soldiers' (or Officers') quarters, and to train everyone in it to faithful service in The Salvation Army.*

6. *We promise, whether together or apart, always to do our utmost as Soldiers of The Salvation Army, and never allow it to be injured or hindered by anyone without doing our best to prevent or overcome such injury or hindrance.*

7. *Should either of us cease to be an efficient Soldier, owing to sickness, death, or any other cause, we engage that the remaining one shall continue to the best of his or her ability to fulfil all these promises.*[40]

In essence, some 125 years later, the articles of marriage have not substantially changed,[41] though their length and form of expression is significantly different.

After the ceremony the General made another speech, the half of which could not be contained in Thursday's edition of *The War Cry* (the paper was issued twice weekly in those days), spilling over into Saturday's columns (21 October), together with speeches from both Mrs Booth and Commissioner Railton.

That the public regarded the Army as a 'nine days wonder' in those early years was highlighted to even greater effect by the General:

'Let me say that in this union we have here this morning a further pledge and guarantee as to the permanence and perpetuity of this movement. People are asking in all directions, "How long will it last?" and "when will it come to an end?" and saying "if we could only be sure that the movement would go on and go forward, we would give it our good word," and some of them say they would also give it their money. Now, I say, there is no guarantee like flesh and blood. Well, this flesh and blood guarantee you have in this union, this morning consummated between these two persons, one of whom is as well known, or nearly so, to The Salvation Army, as I am myself. ...

'People are saying, "What will happen when the General is gone?"' (He was 53 at this stage.) 'By the blessing of God, although the Generalship of the Army is in no sense hereditary, and it is not contemplated to make it such, in the possibilities and probabilities happening in this direction, after the General, the son would step into his place; and, should he do so, there would rally round him, I believe, as cordially and as thoroughly the hearts of the thousands and tens of thousands composing this organization as they have rallied round me. (Loud volley.) Therefore I say there is no immediate need for fear. ...

'You have also in this union a further guarantee of the spirit, the Army spirit, the war spirit in which the movement has been carried on. We all know that the great fear about movements is the life going out of them ... an organization, no matter how capable may be its leaders, and no matter how clever may be its theology, if the life is gone out of it, it is of no use to God or man. ...When the spirit, the life of The Salvation Army goes out of it, I pray that God may bury it, and if I am allowed to come down again I will come to the funeral. ...'

The length of the proceedings may be judged by the fact that 'Mr RAILTON was here asked to speak, but as many were leaving deferred his remarks till a later period. The collection was then made, which will go towards the deficiency of the purchase of the Grecian Theatre, the debt on which, said the General, is crippling us in all directions.' (To Dr Soper's astonishment more than one thousand pounds was that day raised towards the debt.)[38]

After 'Miss BOOTH from Paris' had spoken on behalf of her new sister-in-law – 'one of the first *War Cry* sellers in the streets of Paris' – the General introduced his own wife, Mrs Booth:

'The GENERAL: I feel as if it were our wedding-day over again. It is twenty-seven years since we were wed, and I feel as much like being married today as I did then. (Laughter.) Oh, I enjoy life, and so would you, ever so much, if you were to get properly saved. (Volley.)

'Mrs. BOOTH: Yes, twenty-seven years.

'The GENERAL: You are as fond of me as ever, are you not? (Loud laughter.)

'Mrs. BOOTH: Well, I can say this much, that the highest happiness I can wish to my beloved children, is that they may realise as thorough a union, and realise as much blessing in this union, as the Lord has vouchsafed to us in ours. And if He will do that for them, I will be content, so far as they are individually concerned; but I covet for them that, where I have been the mother of hundreds of spiritual children, that she may be the mother of thousands (cheers), and I covet for my son that whereas the Lord has blessed his father to the salvation of thousands, He may bless him to tens of thousands!'

It was left to the effervescent Commissioner Railton to bring the lengthily entertaining proceedings to a suitably rousing close by leading the great congregation in the singing of 'All hail the power of Jesus' name'.

The wedding luncheon over, the newly-weds were driven in a four-wheeler by 'the Salvationist cabman' to catch the train for Tunbridge Wells, en route to Southborough. The rush hour was in full spate and home-going City gentlemen reading accounts of the wedding in the evening papers surrounded the couple (in those days the Army was 'news' and a full table of reporters below the platform could be relied on at any big event[42]). Fortunately, to the honeymooners' relief, none of their fellow travellers appeared to recognise them.[38] Seldom, if ever, again would the new Mrs Booth be able to rely on such anonymity.

CHAPTER 8

SEPARATE SPRINGS AND SEPARATE MATTRESSES

THE regulation annual holiday for Salvation Army officers in 1882 was 14 days[38] and the Chief of the Staff made no exception for his own honeymoon. Half a century later his bride wrote: 'I wish it were in my power to tell our love story, to describe something of the bliss of our forty-eight years of oneness of heart and the forty-seven years of honeymoon, for our love knew no waning; its fire burned brightly to the last moment of his earthly life. ... In our union we realised, in small measure, perhaps, but with a true reality, something of the Heavenly Father's plan for His people. "Husbands, love your wives even as Christ also loved the Church and gave Himself for it" (Ephesians 5:25).'

Their own home at 32 Castlewood Road[38] not being immediately ready for occupation, they spent a little over a week with Bramwell's parents at nearby 114 Clapton Common. The proximity of the two properties was something Florence had quickly to come to terms with. On 3 November she confided to her diary: 'I moved in today. Tonight I am tired and melancholy. My love has gone to 114 to do business. He has to go every night, and will have to, I expect. I see very little of him ... though he is a greater darling than ever. He has such a weight on his shoulders ... I never mean to let him see that I am down or weary if I can possibly help it. ... This little house is delightful.'[4 & 43]

Most of their furniture was a wedding present from Bramwell's parents, and so anxious was the Army Mother that her son's home should set an example of unworldly simplicity to other young Salvationists that she gave the furniture dealers orders to remove the mirrors from the wardrobe doors and the dining room sideboard. Puzzled, Florence wondered whether her mother-in-law felt the mirrors would be a temptation to the young bride's vanity, but was reassured by the fact that the dressing table's looking glass was allowed to remain. Mrs Booth believed 'good things were always more economical'[44] – she disliked veneer, or anything showy for show's sake. The mahogany dining table,[4] bought very cheaply,[44] was still doing splendid service in the family home of the early1980s when, as the Army's press officer, I escorted visiting journalists to interview Florence and Bramwell's celebrity of an eldest daughter, Commissioner Catherine Bramwell-Booth, then approaching her hundredth birthday. Later, helping her prepare her poems for publication, I frequently lunched – and sometimes breakfasted – at that same multi-leafed mahogany table. Its rounded ends were of particular importance to the Army Mother, having 'no corners for the babies to knock their heads on'.[44]

The expense saved on the purchase of the table was, at her insistence, put towards the maple bedroom suite,[4] which included a bed, long enough at six foot six inches for Bramwell to 'stretch' in. Furthermore, this 'monster' (as their future first-born would describe it) was six foot wide, fitted with separate springs and separate mattresses, affording the pair the minimum disturbance from collateral restlessness.[44] It was money well spent. Assuming that the pregnancy went full term, their first child (like her father before her) was conceived during the honeymoon. But the remaining six were almost certainly conceived in the technologically advanced milieu afforded by that 'monster' bed.

Florence was no less ahead of her time in her views on sexual intimacy, asserting at the age of 74: 'I do not believe that God ordered the physical union in marriage for one purpose only, the multiplying of the race. What S. D. Gordon calls "that hallowed function of nature" may also be the purest expression of hallowed

54

Cover picture and (inset) Florence in her middle years

From top left: Bramwell Booth in 1882, the year of his marriage to Florence; Florence with baby Catherine, 1884; Bramwell, Florence and their family 1890 – Catherine holding a picture of her grandmamma, 'The Army Mother'

Bramwell and Florence Booth with their family, 9 June 1890 – Mary holding Papa's ear trumpet; Catherine seated; Miriam standing with Mama

Florence with her five eldest children, Christmas 1891: (left to right) Mary and
Catherine (standing); Miriam, baby Olive and Bernard

love. Love and lust can never mean the same thing, yet lust I fear does sometimes intrude in marriage, and then love is driven away.

'What clear recollections are retained of that first home which I entered as a bride and where I bore the beautiful name of wife. Our own home! This seemed just a natural thing at the time, but it has brought so much joy to me to realise that this is the plan which our Father God has arranged for His children, that a man should "leave his father and his mother" and choose his partner, and these two in their turn become the responsible heads of a new family.

'There seems so much that threatens the well-being of families in these days that I earnestly hope this narrative of a happy family such as ours may be of some help to the young people who are making, or who are about to make, this important experiment. But that is not the right word. An adventure others have called it, but marriage is much more than either. It is a new state, a new life. I write, of course, of true marriage, of a contract to which the threefold nature, heart, mind, and body, of each of the contracting parties assents.

'Our married life was happy (Oh, that I could describe how happy) because it was the outcome of true love, love to God and love to one another, each esteeming and desiring and loving the other for himself and herself alone. I think a more selfless man than Bramwell Booth could not be. He lived for those he loved, his parents, his brothers, his sisters, and his friends, and for me. A phrase in one of his letters to me two years after our union is a true description of his devotion. "Love is a weak word for all the service and adoration of my heart which you command."'[4]

Yet the early days of her marriage were not without their frustrations for Florence, undomesticated as she was. Hundreds of pounds had been spent on her education, yet nothing had been done to prepare her for the task of housekeeping. She had gained the impression that a store cupboard was there to be filled. Not being accustomed to the daily calls of trades people and having no idea, for instance, how far a pound of rice would go, in placing her first grocery order she judged the quantity by the price and was supplied with enough rice to last a year.[38]

A mere four years had elapsed since The Christian Mission had evolved into The Salvation Army, and, in Bramwell's words, 'We had to build the ship while we were at sea, and not only build the ship, but master the laws of navigation, and not only master the laws of navigation, but hammer sense into a strangely assorted crew!'[45]

A basic navigational law of the Movement, pre-dating even the landmark change of name, was the recognition that 'there is neither ... male nor female; for you are all one in Christ Jesus' (Galatians 3:28 *RSV*). Marriage to Bramwell, therefore, by no means meant that Florence's active officership was to be forfeited for domestic bliss. Young Christian that she was in this equally young Army, there was urgent need for her gifts to be discovered and developed and deployed. Whether the idea had been hatched by her parents-in-law, or the literary-minded George Scott Railton, or by Bramwell himself, she was quickly put to preparing a harmony of the Gospels for *The Salvation Soldiers' Guide*, a book of Bible readings for morning and evening throughout the year. 'It was a time of blessing and enrichment and brought to me an insight into the harmony of the whole Bible which made it a new Book,' she said.

Meanwhile, as Bramwell and his father were attempting to 'hammer sense' into the rest of the 'strangely assorted crew', the laws of navigation were being overtaken by the laws of Nature at 32 Castlewood Road.

'When we realised that God had blessed our union with the gift of a little child, I needed to adjust my thoughts,' wrote Florence. 'I had not loved children or had any desire for them, and before our firstborn came I rather shrank from the responsibility. I read that "The qualities *actively exercised* by the mother, rather than those possessed, are those which descend to the offspring by the laws of heredity." This made me fear that my life at that time was *too quiet*. I grew wiser later on, and learned to value greatly the comparative rest that necessarily comes into the most active life before the birth of a child.'[38]

Comparative rest not withstanding, four months into her pregnancy Florence travelled to France to supervise translation work being undertaken for the Army by her French teacher from school days. Separated from Bramwell for the first time since their marriage, she felt 'very lost and lonely', and although she conducted a Sunday's meetings in Paris on her way home, the absence of Katie, facing the most extreme persecution in Switzerland, only added to Florence's loneliness.[38]

The third Catherine Booth was born on 20 July 1883. 'What love and delight came with her as she was placed in my arms!' remembers Florence.

'There was perhaps some degree of disappointment in his family that this was a girl,' commented the girl herself 50 years later, 'but her father was too immersed in work to be anything but grateful that all was well, and boy or girl of his would surely be of some help to the "Concern" one day.'[46] At this historic moment the disappointed ones in his family would have done well to remember that basic navigational law of the Army that 'there is neither ... male nor female; for you are all one in Christ Jesus' (Galatians 3:28 *RSV*).

The first Catherine Booth, sensing these unspoken thoughts, gave the child a special blessing. 'She seems to be the image of her father, of which Florrie says she is very glad,' she wrote to the second Catherine Booth. 'It is a dear little duck, just a lovable baby.'[38]

Addressing a conference of Salvation Army social workers in 1921 on 'The Care and Training of Children', she who 'had not loved children or had any desire for them' revealed the philosophy the upbringing of her own seven children had instilled in her: 'God's plan for children is that their mother should be young with them.' (Florence was not yet 22 when Catherine was born.) 'Though human beings are so much alike, it is the differences that are vital. This is especially so with children; and this is why we cannot deal with children except individually. ...

'If you want a clever child, he or she must have plenty to do, plenty to make ... Every child possesses a creative instinct in one direction or another: it is very important that this should be encouraged and developed ... A child must not only have something to do, something to make: there must be someone to admire the finished work. ...'[47]

The *Daily Telegraph* of 23 October 1883 described 'The Salvation Army Christening' – the occasion when the Founder dedicated his first grandchild in the presence of her parents and a typically lively Army congregation – declaring: 'It is the principle of The Salvation Army that everything we have or possess belongs to God; that the misery of the world commenced with rebellion against God and in believing that we could manage better for ourselves than God could manage for us. We hold it to be a principle of true godliness, true religion, that we should go back to God and give Him our hearts, our lives, and all we possess. This father and mother are here tonight carrying out that principle, and in the presence of this congregation and before all the holy angels, bring the dearest, choicest treasure with which God has entrusted them, and offer this dear precious child up to Him, and engage that they will train, and nurture, and strengthen it to be not only a child but a servant of the living God, and a good Soldier of Jesus Christ, to fight His battles and take His lot.'

The dedication ceremony took place at Exeter Hall in The Strand on Monday evening 22 October. 'Are you willing,' the General asked Bramwell, 'that this dear child of yours shall be thus consecrated, and will you engage to train it for His service?' Bramwell assured his 'dear General' that he was. Then it was the young mother's turn.

'Are you willing, my dear girl, that your child shall be consecrated to the service of the living God after the fashion I have described, and will you join with your dear husband in keeping it from everything in the shape of strong drink, tobacco, or finery, or wealth, or hurtful reading, or dangerous acquaintance, or any other thing that would be likely to interfere with the effect of such training and such education?'

Florence promised with joy to train 'it' for The Salvation Army and God alone, and 'to do my very utmost to make her understand from the commencement that that is the life she should share, and that that will be sufficient for her'.

Taking his first grandchild in his arms the General declared: 'In the name of The Salvation Army, in the name of the God of The Salvation Army, I take this child and present it to Him ... and I pray that Catherine Booth may be a true saint, a real servant, and a bold and courageous soldier in The Salvation Army, having grace not only to make her own title and election sure, but to secure for a great multitude of other people rescue from misery and sorrow here and everlasting death hereafter. Take it, mother, take it. The father will help you to train it for God and for The Salvation Army.'[48]

As the eldest of the five girls and two boys born to Florence and Bramwell, Catherine has left on record glimpses of how seriously her parents took these vows: 'Family prayers were no formality. We children were allowed to bring any instruments we could play; a drum and a triangle for the "little ones". The custom was to sing the same song for a week so that we might learn the words; the verses were read out for the benefit of those who could not yet read. When, not having gone to the office so early as usual, [our father] instead of our mother took family prayers, one of the younger ones sat on his knee, and he made remarks about the Bible portion as he read, which explained and applied it. Often he addressed his comments to the child on his knee, who sometimes commented too. ...

'Our mother and father were absolutely one in our eyes. I do not remember witnessing a difference of opinion between them on any matter in our presence as children; it became a joke that whichever you asked first about a matter would say, "What does Mama say?" or *vice versa*. He had a way of inspiring our best effort, "to please Mama": as she had the strongest plea, "it would please Papa". ...

'Everything at home was subordinate to the Army's interests. How easily we might have come to hate it! It robbed us of so much, especially of those two beloved ones, and there were many things we must not do, nor have: "it would not be Army." But instead we loved it, and first at the corps, where all of us became soldiers as soon as we were old enough, and later as officers, we learned to regard it as our chief love.'[49]

To this day I cherish an aural (rather than visual) memory from my mid-1980s visits to North Court, the home of Florence and Bramwell's three remaining daughters. The breakfast gong had sounded. On arrival in the dining room, one helped oneself to the home-baked bread, the Stilton cheese and the homemade marmalade gracing the aforementioned (mirror-less) sideboard; then, having said one's own grace, custom allowed one to commence feasting without further ado. On this particular morning I became aware of someone whistling a 'jolly' tune ('jolly' was an adjective much in use by that generation of Booths, traceable, I suspect, to Bramwell himself). The tune was the one associated with the words:

> My sins rose as high as a mountain,
> They all disappeared in the fountain,
> He wrote my name down
> For a palace and crown,
> Bless his dear name, I'm free.

The whistling being accompanied by the steady hum of the stair lift, I realised it must be coming from the lips of one of 'the sisters' – Catherine, Olive or Dora – descending to break her fast. Sure enough Dora appeared – the family's hewer of wood and drawer of water – bent over a walking stick, but giving just as much early morning testimony to the joy of her salvation as she had learnt to do in childhood family prayers more than 90 years earlier.

Within months of Catherine's birth Florence's diary reveals that she was asking God to find her a particular 'corner in His vineyard'. Presumably her work on *The Salvation Soldiers' Guide* had by then been completed.

'December 23, 1883: I was blessed last Sunday morning and am determined to trust God more to bring my feet into the "right place". Perhaps I am not called to preach in public or to help anybody in particular. … I had a talk with dear Mama [Mrs Booth] and she said I must feel that this "32" is my sphere for the present, and I must find my interest in it and learn of God. …'

Then this from the girl who, until she herself was 18, had resented any approach by religious folk hoping to influence her: 'I want to be able to bring baby up wholly for the Lord. … I do pray that she may be impressed with the reality of all she sees and hears of religion.'[50]

One of three surviving unedited diaries sheds precious light on the young wife's struggles not only to discern God's plan for her, but, more crucially perhaps, to please her mother-in-law with regard to the upbringing of her children. Let these entries bring to a close this chapter on Florence's early experience of marriage and motherhood:

'January 11, 1885: Mama talked to us after dinner. Impossible it seems almost to come to any understanding – but will buckle to, to try again. God will surely help. It makes me so utterly wretched. Humanly speaking [it] takes all the joy out of precious baby.'

'January 13, 1885: … the devil too has been at me all day. So downhearted and melancholy I feel about Mama's feelings about baby, but God means me to learn some lessons from it. I will learn. My soul cries out for more of <u>God</u> and to <u>know</u> Jesus and his power. I <u>am going</u> forward. This shall be the very best year.'

'April 17, 1885: Bramwell told me about a conversation with the General about the baby and her hair and dress etc.'

'June 3, 1885: Blaina. A beautiful day. … Read 1 Deuteronomy – Moses' words: "Ye shall not be afraid of the face of man for the judgement is God's." This is just what I need. I feel I need more and more saving from the opinion of those I love and honour. God has delivered me from other fear, but this also must go if the works of the Spirit are to be brought forth in me.

Eliza Armstrong* bought.'

'June 4, 1885: 'Another beautiful day. The babies out all day – Catherine with her wheelbarrow and digging in the beds etc.

Cut out 4 flannel garments for Cath.

Telegram from B[ramwell] saying business with Rebecca* and purchase of girls etc satisfactorily concluded.
Had a sweet time with the Lord – Hebrews and Deuteronomy. No condemnation now I dread.
Eliza Armstrong* to Paris.'

*The references to Eliza Armstrong and Rebecca will become clear in Chapter 10.

CHAPTER 9

KEEPING OFF THE LAUNDRY WORK

A YEAR or two before Bramwell's mother entered into that confident liaison with the Almighty to find her eldest son a wife, baker's wife Mrs Elizabeth Cottrill came to one of her Whitechapel holiness meetings. A resident of Christian Street, she had until then been only a 'formal Christian', she explained in 1921 at the age of 81 years. 'At the penitent form I took the feather out of my hat and came home like a drowned rat, crying and weeping for joy, and from that day I went forward, not to *sing* "Rescue the Perishing", but to do it!'

Evidently there was more to Elizabeth Cottrill's profession of faith than the giving-up of feathers, for: 'I said, "Lord, I'll do whatever you want," and I went visiting lodging-houses and thieves' kitchens. ... I was sent to deal with those at the penitent form, and one snowy February night a girl penitent asked, "How can I be a Christian – the life I'm living?" I said, "You must give up that life." It was very late that night, 10 to 11, when she gave her heart to God.

'I took her down to a home where they'd taken such girls before, but the matron looked out of the window and said, "I can't take girls in at this hour. We don't keep open all night." Then I went to a coffee-house. The charge was 2s 6d, and I only had 1s, and they would not trust me till the morning. I tried another, and was told, "We don't take females." So I said, *"I'll* take her home." I lived at No.1 Christian Street, Commercial Road, next door to a pawnbroker's. It was nearly 12, and my husband and six children were asleep. I gave her some supper – coffee and a little bit of cold meat, and bread and butter. I didn't want any myself. I wanted to get to bed. I was full of prayer and thankfulness, thinking about her broken-hearted mother and how glad she'd be.

'I made her up a bed in the kitchen on some chairs with old coats and dresses – the best I could get without waking the others. I couldn't undress her. She was a clean girl. She had run away from her home near Brighton with another girl, expecting to find London streets paved with gold. They went to the Tower Hill to see the soldiers, imagining they'd find a husband straight away, but only got into trouble. I took her home the next day. I said, "You must ask your mother's forgiveness, and if she won't take you in I'll bring you back." Of course, her mother *did* take her in, only too thankful to see her safe. After this, the soul-saving work amongst these girls went on, and I would get four and even eight in my little place. So I began to pray for a bigger house.'[51]

This incident having taken place in 1881,[52] Mrs Cottrill's lesson in persistent prayer proved to be a lengthy one. It was not until a spring morning in 1884 that 'Mr Bramwell' was disturbed in his office at 101 Queen Victoria Street by a tearful Mrs Cottrill. 'Her husband – good, long-suffering man – could stand these strange lodgers no longer. They upset the house; it was bad for the children. They must go, and go quickly – and oh! What should she do?

'"Tell your husband I perfectly understand," replied the young Chief of the Staff, taking in the domestic situation immediately. "He is quite right. We will do something at once, Mrs Cottrill."'[53]

'The Lord answered my prayers,' her memoirs continue. 'Mr Bramwell Booth had said, "Look for some rooms," but nobody would let rooms for that purpose. I hunted and hunted in vain. Then, walking along Hanbury Street one day, praying as I went, I said: "Lord, the earth is thine, and the fullness thereof. Oh do let me have a house! You know these dear girls are thy children." Then, when I'd cast it on him, I thought: "I'll go home and have a cup of tea." But at that moment I lifted my eyes and saw an empty house, and a notice up, "This house to let." I forgot my tea, and went to inquire.

'The agent was in the same street, and a clerk showed me over, and I saw it would be suitable. But the rent was 25s. I said, "Will you let me have it for £1?"' (A good East-Ender was Mrs Cottrill!) 'Ever so many Jews were after it and ready to pay the 25s. The Rev William Tyler, Congregational, was the landlord, and when he understood he said, "Let this woman have it for £1. I wish there were a few more who had such a heart towards the poor girls." But he said to me, "Don't let there be any tambourines, because I may be preaching!" His church was next door. He gave me 10s to get the girls something to eat. You see, God *does* answer prayer. I got the right sort of landlord!

'The Army Mother' (as Mrs Catherine Booth had come to be known) 'went to a sale and got four single beds and some other things. There was a double bedstead in the lot, and I said, "Let me buy that for myself," but she insisted on giving it to me. ... I loved her so much. She was so thoughtful and so careful. ... She taught me so much, and did her utmost to build me up. Mr Bramwell let me have some old chairs from the Grecian Theatre (which had just been taken over), and I got the girls to scrub the house down and to scrub the chairs. We made bed-ticks and pillow-cases out of old cotton skirts, and I stuffed them with wool and paper the girls had cut up. Sometimes I'd put four of those pillows together to make an extra bed. I begged clothes of all I knew. Often I had to rig a girl up before she could be put to bed. They were smart outside, but – *underneath*!

'Some of the men who were after the girls I'd got would wait for me, and get hold of my bonnet and drag it off; or they'd throw me into a passage; or kick me in the shins, and when a man is wearing blucher boots they can give a bad kick. My husband used to say, "I shall have you killed one of these days."'[51] But in spite of such daily hazards, Mrs Cottrill was to live to the age of 87.

Meanwhile the Hanbury Street cottage rental posed no small problem in the mind of Bramwell Booth. Should the Army take on rescue work officially?[54] Since abandoning soup kitchens and food shops in the mid-1870s, its work had been solely evangelical. But these girls were coming to its penitent forms as a direct *result* of its evangelism. Should not they then be helped? Yet how was this new undertaking to be financed?

In some measure the problem presented its own answer. Writing of the rescue work less than four years later, a Salvationist journalist pointed out: 'It is all very well to rejoice that Middlesbrough's makes our 12th Army rescue home. We thank God for every one of the hundreds snatched from a life of infamy, touched, softened, *saved* through our rescue workers. But to ensure a girl's being "saved to stay", you must also be able to ensure her an honest livelihood.'[55]

Whether it was this kind of psychology, or the force of economic necessity, or a blend of both that led her to it, Elizabeth Cottrill 'toiled all her spare time to get them into situations [employment], sometimes walking many miles a day. Red jerseys were just being introduced as uniform and Mrs Cottrill secured the marking of these with "The Salvation Army" in yellow wool. The girls were taught to do this in cross-stitch, and 3s 6d per dozen was thus earned. A little washing was secured for others to do, and so the rent was paid and food procured.'[51]

With the hindsight of the years, this simple step was to be described in 1928 as 'another of those foundation axioms' of Salvation Army social work – 'that every woman and girl capable of doing so should help towards the cost of her own redemption'.[56]

Seeing the hand of the Lord in it all, Bramwell took oversight of this work on 22 May 1884.[57] Four days later, when Elizabeth Sapsworth, 'a Clapton lady of middle age and independent means, was waiting on the steps of Clapton Congress Hall, she had a five-pound note thrust into her hands by the young Chief of the Staff, with instructions to go and finance the work and keep the books. ... "She had a brain like a statesman's for strength and comprehensiveness,"' Florence was later to write of this 'cultured, methodical scholar in Greek, Hebrew and mathematics',[58] and now was added to her other qualifications that of being The Salvation Army's first rescue officer – before she had even been made a

66

soldier![59] At this stage, however, Florence and Miss Sapsworth had yet to meet. Wrote Florence:

'On June 30, 1884 I went to Ireland ... and assisted in a series of meetings, some public, when the theme was holiness, and some drawing-room meetings, when we explained the work of The Salvation Army. ...This was the first separation from baby Catherine, and the homecoming was delightful.

'On returning from Ireland I heard of the work which had begun in the East End of London among outcast girls. ... The Founder said: "Flo had better go down and see what she can do in her spare time. Let her superintend."

'The next morning, July 18th, I left the trees and greenness of Clapton Common and journeyed by tram to Whitechapel alighting in the High Road to find the cottage in Hanbury Street, a side turning.

'I felt depressed and unhappy. Whitechapel seemed so far away from Castlewood Road for a work which I realised would need daily attention. I felt, too, that I was entirely ignorant of the conditions into which I was to inquire.'[50] Later she was to confess: 'I had not then even realised that there were such people as prostitutes, nor defined to myself what this evil was.'[60]

'Heavy with these thoughts I walked slowly, but was aroused by a blow from a missile hurled at me by a costermonger's boy who had taken a potato from his barrow. The effect was electric. This assault seemed to dispel my fears. I interpreted it to mean opposition and knew that the devil does not waste his ammunition!

'The first days were spent in interviewing those already in the cottage. God had shown me "my corner", but what a very dark and dismal corner it seemed. ... When I heard from the lips of these young girls just in their teens the stories of their destruction; when I understood that women kept houses of ill-fame in which other women were practically prisoners; and that if they were 13 years of age, or if there were reason to believe they had reached that age, the men who destroyed them could not be punished; that for these outcast women there seemed no place of repentance on earth, and the majority, even if they wished to return, were cast out of their homes and no one would give them employment; I felt this was a mystery of iniquity indeed.

'My faith was sorely tried, and but for the opportunity of pouring out my grief at home to one so strong in faith and so full of compassion for the sinful, I wonder what might have become of me. How acute were the contrasts in my life at this time; such bliss at home, the purest love of husband and my darling baby in her cot, and then suddenly these terrible revelations. This underworld seemed indeed a scene of diabolic confusion and darkness.'

Eager to become as knowledgeable as possible upon every aspect of her new work, Florence visited rescue homes run by other organisations, but heard a very discouraging story as to good results. 'Women were kept in these places for one, two, and even three years, and if they failed to run well, were never given a second chance. Bolts and bars, bare dismal rooms, high walls, no occupation but that of laundry work, seemed to explain this discouragement. I could not imagine myself becoming any better for a long stay in similar circumstances. I determined therefore to make, at first, no rules for the refuge. I realised that there is no power in a mere removal from certain circumstances to reform the heart, and especially I felt that what these women most needed was a real home, for they were homeless, and that they needed support in their first efforts to earn their own living and return to respectable society.'[50]

Yet again the 22-year-old was proving to be ahead of her times, and certainly ahead of Miss Ellice Hopkins, 'a lady of perhaps the widest experience in England with this class of women', who was of the opinion that of all the employment open to them, laundry work was best. In her own words, 'As a rule, it stands to reason that the wild restlessness, the lawlessness, the animal passions and excitement of the old street life are best worked off by muscular exertion, and laundry work is on the whole the best and most profitable.'[62]

'We keep *off* the laundry work', insisted Florence, 'because we wish opportunity for more personal influence over the girls.'[63] This personal influence is evidenced in her early experiments with a small group of girls: 'The occupation of a teacher in the scholastic realm is intensely interesting, though I suppose the large classes often make it impossible to follow up closely individual cases, *but the education of heart and conscience is more enthralling still.*[1] ... It was intensely interesting to see the light gradually dawning as the things of God were personally explained. Two officers in charge of the home were with the women all the time. Miss Sapsworth, a lady who lived at Clapton, interested herself in this work, joined The Salvation Army and became my most able helper.' (Presumably Mrs Cottrill was the other 'officer' in these early days.) 'When we visited the refuge we joined the family party and had dinner and tea with the women. They learned many [religious] songs and choruses, for we felt in this way their minds were occupied and any frivolous or hurtful conversation was prevented.'[50]

Another aspect of the enlightened way Florence approached the setting up of the rescue work harks back to Catherine Booth's stipulation of 'no mirrors' in the furnishing of Bramwell and Florence's first married home. In visiting rescue homes run by other organisations 'I found no looking-glasses in any of the apartments used by the women. I decided that the looking-glass for necessary self-inspection exercised no hurtful influence and that Salvation Army homes should not display this lack. The prejudice of some social workers at that time against mirrors was peculiar. [Later] we acquired as a home for women a beautiful house with long mirrors on the panelled wall of the entrance hall and of the drawing room, which was to be used as the work-room. I found that the officer in charge had covered all these fearing a "bad effect on the women". I vetoed this, and several of the visitors who attended the opening were thereupon astonished that the mirrors were permitted to remain in an institution!'[4]

But panelled entrance halls and mirrored drawing rooms were an unimaginable prospect during the first 15 months at the little five-roomed[50] Hanbury Street cottage, with only a kitchen-cum-dining room and small front room on the ground floor, and inadequate sanitary arrangements. Until a public laundry was discovered, where, at a small charge, clothes could be washed, all the washing had to be dried in front of the smoky fire in the living room.[65]

Florence's 'most able helper', Elizabeth Sapsworth, was the sole accountant and cashier, as well as statistician, for the first seven years of the rescue work. Apart from the business routine, her desire to spread the gospel – in spite of the handicap of deafness – found a new fulfilment at the refuge.[58] Miss Sapsworth's statistical skill is revealed in a note in Florence's diary of 12 January 1885, recording that in the first six months the refuge received no fewer than 84 girls, four of them from prison. Twenty-one were still under the care of the refuge or in hospital. Of the 63 who had left, 40 were doing well, one had emigrated, two were happily married, 32 were in domestic employment, five who had been reconciled to their parents were living at home and seven had been passed on to other institutions. Only 12 had returned to their old ways, and four had been lost sight of.

'The large proportion of young girls who come is a hopeful fact, as our chance with these is much greater than with older women, because drink has not such a firm hold on them. I am firmly convinced of the wisdom of leaving them all free to quit the refuge at any moment. Those who do not *desire* to stay are better away. Of the five who have run away *four* have come back to us, literally seeking again a place of repentance, with tears.'[57]

CHAPTER 10

STAFF, SERVANTS AND FAITH HEALING

IN the midst of all this pioneering work Florence was not without her staff problems. Miss Sapsworth may well have been her 'most able helper', but entry upon entry in a sample month of Florence's 1885 diary reveals that her 'most able helper' could also be her most time-consuming problem:

'Friday January 2, 1885: ...Miss Sapsworth ran in 10 minutes before [my] starting, all upset about Mrs Cottrill. It is very difficult to get these two to work together – felt very disheartened. ...

'Saturday January 3, 1885: ... Mrs Cottrill came up to see me in the evening. I fear Miss Sapsworth spoke unwisely and was the most to blame, but unwittingly – her manner is very harsh. ...

'Monday January 5, 1885: ... Very troubled about Miss Sapsworth and Mrs Cottrill. ...

'Wednesday January 7, 1885: ... I called Mother Cottrill out and had a talk which unfortunately did not get finished before the cab came. I am very dissatisfied with her. She has taken Rhoda, whom Miss Sapsworth said could not stay, into her own house. I think she will very likely succeed with her. ...

'Saturday January 10, 1885: Miss Sapsworth came up in the morning. Said she was miserable thinking I had lost confidence in her. Ridiculous reasons. Must try and get her over these <u>little</u> things – How I head my letters etc. Showed her I hope where the mistake lay with Mrs Cottrill. Hope things will be better. ...

'Tuesday February 3, 1885: ...6:30. I put babs to bed – Did accounts. Miss Sapsworth and [Captain] Lacy arrived in trouble. Rose had come to [Miss S's] house saying the Mother [Mrs Cottrill]

71

had turned her out of the Home and said it was not just to send away Susan and keep her. Felt distressed that Mrs C could be so unwise. Wrote for her to come and see me. ...

'Wednesday February 4, 1885: Felt very poorly, in bed, bad cold and cough wrote letters. Mrs C arrived about 11:30. Rose told lies last night. Was dreadfully abusive to the Mother [Mrs Cottrill] and Emily and then went off to Miss Sapsworth on her own account. Mother said – after she had announced her intention of going – If you are going, do not stay to talk so, but go. Mrs C talked about Whitechapel. It is a great pity – fear it will never be put straight. ...

'Thursday February 5, 1885: ... Talked with Miss Sapsworth about Mrs C. Had great difficulty at first, but afterwards arrived at my point. Miss S <u>cannot</u> divest herself of the past. Mrs C went up and kissed and forgave Rose. Rose is tamer and has <u>prayed</u>.'

Lest it should be assumed that such contretemps between Miss Sapsworth and Mrs Cottrill were the sole stuff of Florence's days, a glance at a few of the hurriedly scribbled diary entries in which this minutiae is embedded will quickly establish the pace at which her life was moving:

'Friday January 2, 1885: Rose at ¼ to 7 with babs [Catherine]. Had a nice time with the Lord. It is <u>very</u> cold weather. Baby still poorly. a.m. Did accounts. Wrote Lacy, Didz [one of her aunts], Mr Buckle Southampton, Mr Nobbs.

Left ¼ to 4 for Mrs Walker's [Mrs de Noe Walker – see Chapter 3]' (this is when Miss Sapsworth ran in – see above). 'Arrived at 10 Ovington Gardens about 5. Found Mrs Gibson of Paris and as soon as she left the Countess of Seafield was announced. I wait upstairs – Then had tea with Mrs W and Miss Lees and talked about the refuge. Very good meeting at Denyer Hall. Felt the Lord helped me to speak – talked about Union with God. Place quite full. Told Captain Beattie's wife to go for a rest – the former to take her glass eye out. Slept at Mrs Walker's.

'Saturday January 3, 1885: Left Mrs Walker's at 10 – walked to South Kensington with Miss Roberts, a candidate from the Rink who wants to be passed through as she is unable to keep herself in lodgings much longer and has given up her situation because she could not come to the meetings. Felt she was good but there did not seem to be much in her. Mrs Walker however thinks well of her. Found Bramwell had not arrived at the office. Answer a letter from Mrs Davey, Plymouth, which was awaiting me. Wrote up to Dept about the Candidate. Saw Carleton etc and waited till one – was just going when he arrived. I came home with W. Hodgson, meeting Mrs H. Brought them both home to dinner. They were pleased with babs who was very good. B arrived very starved and cold at 5, having been to Marylebone in an open trap.' (Mrs Cottrill arrives – see above.) 'Poor Annie Lewis is drinking and misbehaving herself in the Whitechapel Road. This is heartbreaking. I hear she called for her clothes just as Mrs C was coming away. I shall hear about this on Monday. Feel dissatisfied very with this day's work. It has slipped away from me. Baby still seems poorly – cannot get rid of this cold.

'Sunday January 4, 1885: Home all day. Very dark fog. Captain Boon at 11a.m. Stayed to dinner. Letters: Mrs Hull, Mrs Bell, Mrs Soule, Mrs Olwen Williams, Mrs Smith – Bristol, Mrs Alderton – Cambridge, Mrs Cox. Went up to Rookwood [home of William and Catherine Booth] to tea. Captain Oliphant there. Returned with us. Had serious talk to Edith and gave her notice. Left her upstairs because she was crying and Bailey found her sound asleep a few minutes after. I am afraid she is sleepy over everything.

'Monday January 5, 1885: To 101 with Bramwell and to stores. Finish shopping at 12. Had 12:30 [daily prayer] with Bramwell then to Whitechapel from Mansion House Underground. Found the girls all praying after dinner. I listened in the inner kitchen. It was beautiful, my heart went out to them. Oh! That they were all true. Alice Shingles is a great disappointment. We decide she must go. Rhoda Durling is all wrong again – she is as weak as water. She and Bessie Poole went out together to get Rhoda's clothes out of pawn and R met someone and went to have a drink. Then declared her intention of walking the streets all night. They lost their way and it was dark. A porter who was a Salvation soldier took Bessie to his mother's house and brought her back to us on Sunday evening after his work was done. Rhoda was found on our doorstep Sunday morning. She is not penitent and we must send her to some stricter home. Very troubled about Miss Sapsworth and Mrs Cottrill. Mr Barlow came just as the girls were finishing tea. I was engaged with Miss Sapsworth so he went in. I found him on his knees listening to the girls praying with tears running out of his eyes. Several prayed and we sung "She only touched the hem of his garment". Then we sat round and Annie Lucas who was back for a holiday spoke. Margaret White and Sarah Ford broke down crying. Amelia Box and Mr B said a few words and prayed with us. I think he was pleased. B and I did not get home until 7. I was very tired. No dinner in the middle of the day' (this in the sixth month of her second pregnancy).

'Wednesday January 7, 1885: Rose 7 with baby. After breakfast saw ironmongery. Measured out calico for servants' sheets. Nailed oilcloth onto Nursery table. Wrote letters: Bristol, Mrs Smith, Mrs Brewer, Mrs Johnson. Had lunch 12 and to 212 [Hanbury Street refuge]. Found Rose had had another fight with Alice and ran off saying she would murder Alice in the meeting even if she did 12 months for it. Saw her and had a very serious talk. Made some impression. She wants to be delivered but says it is impossible she should ever be freed from her temper. Had a nice talk with Susan – and Margaret White who starts for Bristol tomorrow. Captain Streeter came to hold the meeting' (talk with Mother Cottrill – see above). 'Came home with B and General at 6. B went up to Rookwood directly after dinner.

'Saturday January 10, 1885: (more problems with Miss Sapsworth – see above). 'Made babies (*sic*) dress. Sent baby up to dinner at Rookwood Road punctually at one. She stayed all day as B did not come home. Came home quite black and B sent her back to show Ma. Ma did not see her.

'Monday January 12, 1885: Went to refuge in Chief's cab 9:30. Dear Emma in to breakfast and we went round by Congress Hall. Miss S was there – found poor dear Susie Pritchard returned. We were so glad to see her. She says she really found the Saviour when she was with us before and has never missed her prayer at night and before her meals and now has made up her mind to leave this man as he will not marry her, but she cannot stay with us in Whitechapel as he will not leave her alone. A lady? came to choose a girl for a friend of hers – a hard place we fear – but Emma and Constance will go round tomorrow and see after it with mother [Mrs Cottrill]. Took all the morning to see about situations. Then dinner. We had a good prayer time afterwards. Mother, Constance, Alice Lucas and self prayed. Had a little talk to Annie Bishop about sending out her baby to nurse and getting some work but found her heartbroken at the idea. We must struggle on with the baby I suppose. Met Mr Eason at Hackney Station at 3 and went to see over the house. House very suitable – if General approves of locality. Same row as Major Carleton's. Rent £45. Mr Lovegrove. Returned by 4:30. Made out figures of refuge for General at Exeter Hall tonight. Very sorry I cannot go. Farewell of 30 officers for Foreign Service. America principally. Baby such a darling, but it is hard to see so little of her. Edith to Exeter Hall. Baby has been at Rookwood all day – came home at 6 and played with me and "Crook".

'Wednesday January 28, 1885: Esther Walker must go to Wotton N. Edge [sic]. Went to refuge in the morning in B's cab and saw Eliza Bunting – she is very hard. Esther Walker – a precious child. I send her with every confidence. She looked so beautiful. Prayed sweetly. Louisa Greenwood – from Exeter. A curious character, naturally low. Now self-righteous. Told me since her reform all the police officers in Exeter respect her. Think I made some impression on her – she cried. She feels parting with her child – a nice little girl of five. We are putting it in Mr Toy's Orphanage for a while. Tall Emily went out seeking a place. Emily Salamon called in the evening about a situation. Told her to come again tomorrow evening. I do wish I could find someone. She seems to me rather mucky.

'Thursday January 29, 1885: Breakfast at 8. B left 8:34. Wrote: 1 Mrs Fox 2 Mrs Read 3 Captain Carter 4 Mrs Bowen 5 Mrs Onslow

6 Sec B & F Bible Society 7 James [?] Williams Esq 8 Mrs Witney 9 Mrs Kurtz [?] 10 Mrs Richardson 11 Dr May 12 Mrs Sherwood 13 Rebecca 14 Ellen Leader 15 Miss Spearman. Went up to Rookwood to see Ma and Emma. Dinner napkins from Dalstone (*sic*) Sale. Felt very downhearted – but Jesus was all in all. I am getting better to be able to say There's nothing else I seek. Mrs Crick called and I sent her up to see Mama. She approved of her. Worked all the morning at a red dress for precious babs. Edith was tiresome all day. Mama sent over for someone to go to the Congress [Hall] so she went. B 5.30. Boon 8.

'Friday January 30, 1885: Went to meet Mr Eason and looked over house in Stepney Green – Fine large old building – very suitable for our purpose – but rather dilapidated. Situation and immediate surroundings very good – rather far from 272 [Whitechapel Road] – but shut in and nice garden. Took Captain Lacy to see it and she was delighted. B goes to inspect tomorrow afternoon. Had so many thoughts as I went up the steps and into the rooms. I wonder if my work will lie there.

'Had a good afternoon at 212, tho' rather disheartened. Miss Read arrived to interview me for the *War Cry* – my head was very bad so fear we made little out. Had dinner with the girls then saw Ada Brotherton. She is serious at last. Eliza has been a better girl since my last talk. She is weak. Bad news from Catherine Chalk. Also Catherine Jones never went to her situation at all, but writes us from her mother's. Most astonishing! Emily Neville is not satisfactory. Beautiful letter from Rebecca. Saw Sarah Ford. Surely she is to be trusted. Received wire from Dovercourt saying Kate Murray was coming home ill. Only today did we receive letter full of satisfaction from her master! B had a wonderful meeting, the best ever since started in the Congress [Hall]. He regrets moving into the Temple, but it will soon settle down there and be <u>full</u>.

'Monday February 2, 1885: Majors Council, Clapton. Mem: To give order that something must be posted to me every night from the refuge if I have not been there, whether I am expected the next day or not.

'Bad news from refuge by letter. Mrs Greenwood drunk. Bessie Poole bad. Susan insubordinate. Eliza Bunting. Had decided for a long time that something must be done with those who have been with us so long without getting really better. Settled they must pass on for a time at least. I saw <u>Susan Amery</u> [?] who cried very much but did not acknowledge how naughty she had been. Told her she must go to the Infirmary. <u>Mrs Greenwood</u> – Fear she is a poor weak thing. <u>Eliza Bunting</u> – cried very much. <u>Elizabeth Knight</u> – Justified herself at first but afterwards broke down. Was pleased with her and left it undecided. Saw also <u>Elizabeth Chardine</u> and was pleased with her. Also <u>Annie from Witney</u>.

'Had a solemn meeting altogether after dinner and spoke of the departures, also about getting up in the morning and talking at night and sitting together in the Hall. Mrs Reed from Norwood called about starting a house for fallen girls. Dressed up in fur etc. Fear she will not do any good. Too weak. We recommended Mrs Digauce ! as matron for her. Went and came home in B's cab. Arrived home at 4:45 very weary. Lay down. B and Captain Oliphant in to supper from the Council at 10.20. Babs is still poorly.

'Tuesday February 3, 1885: Majors Council, Clapton. Wrote [10 letters – names listed]. Jennie Freeman arrived. We took dear babs out for a little walk. Then had lunch and went to the refuge for the meeting. Mrs Caesar Hawkins arrived. We asked her to come in too. We had a good time – sang 490 – Rock of ages. Read some of Matt XVIII. Mrs H said a few words and we had a very good prayer meeting. Ada Brotherton prayed for salvation and Elizabeth Knight. Left at 5:15. Jennie stayed here to tea. Left 6:30. I put babs to bed. Did accounts.' (Here Miss Sapsworth arrived – see above.)

'Wonderful talk upon Faith Healing at the Council. B and Oliphant came home full of it. Something will come out of it.

'Saturday February 7, 1885: Home all day. Sewed and wrote letters. Went to lunch at Rookwood. Dear Mama very down and worried. Baby up there and stayed all afternoon. B home at 5. Dinner at 6. Went up to Rookwood together. Found baby very poorly again – pale and fretful and coughing much. Brought her home – gave her hot blanket, foment and poultice. She went straight to sleep – was very feverish when we came to bed. Kept the fire up all night and gave her aconite – 4 doses. She slept tolerably well. B very poorly.'

Pursuing in passing one strand of Florence's diary entries at the expense of the fuller picture, we note on several pages references to baby Catherine's, Bramwell's and sometimes Florence's own ill health lying cheek-by-jowl with remarks about faith healing. Yet she seems not to make a connection between the two. Is this because hydropathy has become by now the tried and tested remedy for all her family's ills, or because faith healing is such a new concept to her? Her final entry on the subject may shed some light:

'Friday February 6, 1885: Afternoon Council upon faith healing – B talked splendidly, but on the whole I was not much enlightened. ... Got a blessing in the evening meeting. Trusted God for the gifts <u>necessary</u> to do the refuge work.

'At the close Major Pearson held a faith healing meeting – Mrs Young, Mrs Fry, Major Cadman, Musgrave Brown, Major Keats came forward. Mrs Young said she was better, but it seemed to pass off. Major P brought a little bottle of oil out of his trouser pocket to anoint them. It was all so new that I suppose we were wondering rather than believing. Dear Cadman I shall never forget. He cried and prayed and was anointed. Then rising with his eyes shut – opened his eyes, looked at the wall and, saying "No better", sank on his knees again. This he did four times. Then the General prayed and closed. After the others had been anointed Musgrave Brown <u>was</u> released from pains in his head.

'B had a very good Holiness meeting in the Temple. Very tired.'

CHAPTER 11

A LARGE BLUE HAT AND A RED SILK DRESS

WITHIN months of the May 1884 opening of Hanbury Street refuge, warnings were appearing in *The War Cry* to the following effect: 'IMPORTANT! Captains must not send any cases to The Salvation Army Refuge for Women, Whitechapel, without first ascertaining whether there be room to receive them, as they will have to be sent back, which causes great inconvenience and disappointment to all concerned.'[61]

Reading this, Captain Susan 'Hawker' Jones of Northampton, one of those salt-of-the-earth characters out of which the early-day Salvation Army was built, dutifully contacted the Whitechapel refuge regarding her latest houseguest. She had seen a tall woman in a 'large blue hat with great blue feathers' come into the meeting hall one evening and sit near the door. Her demeanour, as much as her hat, caused the captain to notice Rebecca Jarrett, for she was obviously ill. Before long the hot crowded meeting had its effect and she fainted. 'It was not the preaching that done the work in my poor soul, it was the care and trouble they all took of me,'[66] Rebecca remembered in old age.

A brothel-keeper in her late 30s, she had been introduced by her mother to a life of sexual promiscuity before she was 13 years old. Her father, a well-to-do rope merchant, used to give lectures against 'the drink' in a little hall in the Borough, squandering all his money on 'other women' the while. Finally he left her mother, who, with eight of her 13 children still needing support, soon 'took' to the very drink her husband had preached against. As the youngest child, Rebecca became not only the vehicle through which her mother was able to finance her constant drinking sprees, but also her mother's drinking companion.

By the time she stumbled into Captain Jones's Northampton meeting in November 1884, 'I was too old to be reclaimed, besides, I was almost dying with the drink. Every doctor I went to said, "You must give up the drink!" How could I? It made me have a bit of life. … It was drinking to deaden your feeling, to meet the men. If you were not bright they would not come again. They paid your rent and supported you. No, you must drink, if it finished you up.'[66]

Nursing Rebecca in her own tiny room for several days, Captain Jones was finally given clearance to take her patient to Hanbury Street. Wrote Florence: 'Her very appearance was a challenge to my faith, for the marks of her dissolute life were very plain, the expression of her face almost repulsive, and showed plainly the ascendancy that alcohol had gained over her.'[1] Nevertheless, when Rebecca's crisis point came, after prolonged treatment in the London Hospital,[66] Florence had no qualms about handing baby Catherine into the arms of this 'challenge to her faith', whilst she herself went to make the inevitable soothing cup of tea.[67]

Preserved through family oral history, that detail was not recorded in her diary however:

'Friday January 9, 1885: Rebecca was there [at Hanbury Street], just come in from the hospital. I was _so_ glad to see her. She looks ill and she is still faithless about herself. I _fear_ she will go and yet she _desires_ to be made right. Poor thing, her chains are strong.

'Wednesday January 14, 1885: On coming downstairs found very sad news – a letter from Rebecca saying she could not go on trying this new life any longer and she had made an appointment to meet her brother's man and go back to the old life on Sunday when she saw her mother (it appears she met an old acquaintance of sin and went to drink with him, and though she resisted so far as not to go home, he went and fetched her mother and they met. She did not tell her mother where she was, but said she was living by herself. Her mother said if she was living right and keeping herself honestly, that she would be willing to go into Fulham Infirmary and let the Brothel be given up.).

'I spent the morning with R and God helped me to put it all before her what a clear open door this was from the Lord. We talked and prayed and she wept bitterly until dinner-time (1 o'clock) and she would not decide. Said she would think over it till 2, and then send for and tell me. I sent dinner into her and 2 o'clock passed, and at 2:30 I heard Rebecca had gone upstairs, packing her things to go. I sent the Mother [Cottrill] up, but she came down saying she was determined to go, it was no good. Then although it was meeting time I left the girls and a [Salvation Army] soldier from Clapton and took Mother, Lacy and Miss S upstairs and we told Rebecca we must pray for her once more and put things before her once more. I went up to her and talked awhile, then they began to pray. R would not kneel at first. Then she knelt and sobbed and we prayed on. In the midst Mr Denny and Emma arrived. I was obliged to go down. Mr Denny came in to the girls. We sang and several testified ... Mr Denny said a few words and we had prayer – I and Emma prayed.

'Rebecca came down and sat with Mother. After they went Miss S had a few words with her, but she said "No, I cannot." On going up to say goodbye to her and hearing these words I said we could not allow her to go away telling us and herself that lie – she must go facing the truth, that she turned her back on God and Heaven and deliberately chose sin and hell, and that she would go to hell with her mother's soul and the souls of the poor girls she would get into the brothel and the young men etc. That she must go now telling herself and us the same truth that she would acknowledge when we all stand around the throne.

'Suddenly, to my surprise, for I thought she was lost, she broke down bitterly, said "I will give it all up" and fell down on her knees sobbing. She prayed to God to save, said she would give all up. It seemed almost too good to be true. She prayed on and at

81

last said God had taken her in. I asked her if she would like to see the Mother and Lacy, and they came in. She told them amidst her sobs and I cried for very joy.

'She said she would write to her mother that very night and tell her to come away and leave the brothel. I am now praying God will send along some means of her earning her livelihood. Now this means of earning her living which has served her for 13 years has gone and her mother is with us, her temptations will be much less.'

Of that occasion Florence was later to write: 'When such slaves break away from sin and desire to lead a new life, they have no conception of the extent of their own weakness or the tenacity of the power of sin. To be finally saved they must go on to know "life more abundant", and open their hearts without reserve to the indwelling power of God.'[1]

Two days after having 'cried for very joy' Florence was greeted by another of her prodigals, Annie Lucas, who said with tears: 'I've bad news, dear Mrs Bramwell, Amelia Box 'as run off; she took some things from my missus.' Better news followed when 'dear Mrs Bramwell' saw Rebecca 'who is very happy and said she would not look back now'. The following day, since Bramwell, although 'very poorly', was accompanying 'Mama' to Halifax for a weekend's campaigning, Florence and baby Catherine went to stay with her aunts at Sydenham. Before returning home on Monday evening January 19 she had written to Mrs Josephine Butler, possibly as a direct result of receiving a letter from Rebecca saying she had had a reply from her mother.

The next day Rebecca was again admitted to the London Hospital, where at 4 pm Florence visited her: 'She looks so ill – suffering in her hips,' she remarked, adding: 'Had a nice time.' On Saturday 24 January: 'Received beautiful letter from Rebecca in London Hospital,' who, on Monday 26: 'arrived from the Hospital. She was not happy. Drs told her the disease was in her system though only developed at present in her hip. Nurses did not behave well – said the hospital was more than half full of unfortunates and they were only taking up the room of others who wanted to come in.

'Wrote to Mrs Butler to accept her offer for R. I do hope this is the right thing. ... Rebecca's sad, sad history is so depressing. What is not that man worthy of!'

The following day Rebecca left for Winchester, where she was to be met by Josephine Butler and where she would stay for the foreseeable future. Josephine Butler, wife of Canon George Butler, was a warm friend of the Booths. To her courageous campaign against the Contagious Diseases Acts[68] and her staunch advocacy of Katie during her imprisonment in Switzerland[69] would shortly be added firm support for the Army's spirited stance against sexual trafficking in under-age girls – a stance in no small measure hastened by the arrival of Rebecca Jarrett on the Butlers' doorstep on Tuesday 27 January 1885.

An 1871 Royal Commission had reported: 'The traffic in children for infamous purposes is notoriously considerable in London and other large towns. We think that a child of 12 can hardly be deemed capable of giving consent and should not have the power of yielding up her person. We therefore recommend the absolute protection of female children to the age of 14 years.' The age of consent had eventually been raised – to 13, not 14 – but until 1875 any girl over the age of 12 was regarded by English law as a consenting adult in sexual intercourse.[70]

In the six months the now 23-year-old Florence had been responsible for the Army's rescue work, she had not only discovered 'there were such people as prostitutes'[60] but that many of them were mere children, '*old* in depravity at fifteen, at thirteen, at eleven'[64] who 'were being entrapped by a vicious network of carefully devised agencies ...' She discovered 'that there existed a regular traffic in these girls; that it had widespread ramifications, both in England and on the Continent; that it was maintained by the most atrocious fraud and villainy, and involved such anguish and degradation as, in her opinion, could not be matched by any trade in human beings known to history.'

Continued Bramwell, onto whom in despair she unloaded these discoveries: 'Those hideous facts greatly affected her, and during the first year or two of our married life, the skies were often overcast on this account. Where there should have been smiles and brightness there were often tears and sorrow. Thinking of the miseries of these poor creatures, [she] cried herself to sleep night after night. She told me of the most harrowing incidents which had come to her knowledge. I tried to comfort her by suggesting that the stories were probably exaggerated; that the credibility of these folks was not to be trusted too readily, and so on. But, presently yielding to her entreaties, I said that I would look into the matter for myself. I made certain inquiries and interviewed one or two people. Among the latter was the then Chamberlain of the City of London, Mr Benjamin Scott, who, in association with Mrs Josephine Butler, had been attacking the Contagious Diseases Acts then in force. He said that he could well believe all that I heard from my wife, that it was a disgrace to civilization, and that some of the police winked at the betrayers and procurers. He expressed in his gentle, courteous way that something would be done. I answered him with emphasis that something would!'

One could be forgiven for assuming The Girl in the Red Dress was a portrait by Vermeer in the tradition of his *Girl with a Pearl Earring* and *The Girl with the Red Hat*. In fact the Red Dress belonged not to the 17th century, but to the 19th, and, such was the plight of its wearer, she would certainly have identified more readily with the artist's earlier picture of *The Procuress*. Responding to an advertisement for a general servant, the 17-year-old had travelled from the country to London, only to find herself trapped in a brothel. The mistress urged her with increasing force to be a 'lady' like the others in the house, giving her the red silk dress and compelling her to visit a certain music hall in her company. Escape seemed impossible, but amid her alarm and agitation the girl remembered attending Salvation Army meetings in her home town, and that in her box was a little red song book on the cover of which was the London headquarters address. Slipping out of the house at four o'clock in the morning, she walked from Pimlico to Queen Victoria Street, having asked directions from a policeman, and was found, still clutching the song book, outside headquarters when the gate was unlocked at seven.

'The story was hard to believe,' remembered Bramwell, 'but there was the girl ... and there, moreover, was the dress, which obviously was not such as a mistress would provide for a domestic servant.' An officer was sent at once to the address from which she said she had escaped. At first the residents claimed to know nothing about her, but when the caller revealed himself to be an officer of The Salvation Army, and that the Army already had the girl under its protection, they handed her box over to him, confirming the story.

'The incident made a great impression on me,' confessed Florence's young husband, 'an impression which was deepened further when a number of girls were brought up from Whitechapel by [my wife], and I had the opportunity of questioning them. One of them, about 14 years old, manifestly enceinte, told a terrible story of how she had been met in the street by a very "nice" woman, taken to a music hall, persuaded to meet her "friend" again, and so dragged into virtual imprisonment and the last outrage. All this caused me no little suffering and I resolved – and recorded my resolve on paper – that no matter what the consequences might be, I would do all I could to stop these abominations, to rouse public opinion, to agitate for the improvement of the law, to bring to justice the adulterers and murderers of innocence, and to make a way of escape for the victims.'[68]

On Tuesday 10 March 'Mrs Bramwell' went to St George's House to see Mrs Ann Jarrett but failed to find her. Instead, 'Met a mad man in the porch.' Meanwhile, Ann Jarrett's daughter, under the kindly influence of Canon and Mrs Butler of Winchester, was using the last £30 from her former life towards setting up, with the help of many friends, a tiny rescue home of her own in Winchester. This was to be the answer to Florence's prayer of 14 January that God would send along some means of Rebecca earning her livelihood.

On 7 April Florence received word that 'dear Mama' (her stepmother, Mary Levick Soper) was very ill with an attack of erysipelas, and though Florence longed to go to Blaina, she was obliged instead to celebrate the General's 56th birthday by joining with the rest of the family for dinner at Mrs Onslow's. At 8pm on Saturday 11, a telegram announced: 'Entering the gates since morning. Only at perfect rest at six this evening.' Florence was devastated.

'I ought to have expected it but it seemed as sudden as if I had never heard. I could not give her one kiss or have one look or be by dearest Papa a minute. Bramwell would have gone down but he could not catch the last train – 9:15 from Paddington. He says he will go on Monday. B went up to Rookwood and Annie Lucas and Anna Skerritt arrived. I had to see them. Was longing to be alone to cry.'

The following day Florence telegraphed home to say Bramwell would come on Monday, but after tea 'Mama [Bramwell's] very afraid of infection. General also against it, so decided not. I feel fearfully low and longed intensely to go. Love to Papa has come over me again like a wave.'

'Monday, April 13, 1885: Letter from the dearest Father giving full particulars of dearest Mother's illness and death. Felt it would almost break my heart as B read it. Baby sitting at table cried because I cried. I kissed her and sent her upstairs. What can she know of death! What will she ever know of the dear one who loved her so and did so much for her? The little drawers [pants] for the summer will be at Blaina unfinished. Bramwell obliged to leave for the city and Miss Sapsworth called, so again had to leave my tears and my sorrow for the Kingdom's sake.

'Wednesday, April 15, 1885: Went to Dalston with Bailey and Babs in train to order wreath of flowers for Babs to send to the precious one at Blaina. Lilies of the Valley over. ...

'Friday, April 17, 1885: ... Bramwell missed his train at 5:45 for Cardiff through the nastiness of an Inspector. He went to take his Holiness Meeting, coming home soon after ten. ...

'Saturday, April 18, 1885: Sent my precious love off [to Blaina] at 4:30am. He is far from well, God keep him. ... Mrs Walker ...

Miss Bennett ... Miss Sapsworth with Capt and Lieut ... Had tea and then prayer. Read 1 Corinthians 12. Said a few words – Oh! How I wish I were a talker that could inspire people. ... Made bed in the bassinette and filled the basket.'

On Monday 20th Bramwell arrived home from Blaina, presumably having attended the funeral.

'Tuesday, April 21, 1885: Made white walking dress for baby at the machine. Obliged to call for Mrs Crick [midwife] after tea. Baby born at 1:15 on Wednesday morning, April 22 1885.'

She was called Mary, of course, after the step-grandmother she would never now know, and also after her great-grandmother Booth. There are no more diary entries until nine days later, when Florence 'got out and had bed made'. The following day she 'sat up in chair bed'. But it was not until 18 days after the birth that Florence 'came down stairs to dinner'. Six days later Rebecca arrived:

'Saturday, May 16, 1885: Rebecca came at 12. Has been missioning in Portsmouth and became discouraged through losing a woman. ... The Winchester cottage work is too much for her single-handed. I trust she will hold on until I can get our house and have her.

'Went for a drive at 2.30 taking her with Hicks and the two babies with us. Just as we were starting Dr and Mrs Heywood Smith drove up.'

The good doctor, a gynaecologist from the City of London Lying-in Hospital,[75] might well have been making a professional call on the new mother, but the fact of his converging upon Castlewood Road on the same day as Rebecca was not without significance, as we shall discover in due course.

In the meantime Rebecca had tried to make her Winchester home as attractive as when keeping a house for the opposite purpose. Her principal aim was to reach girls under 14, and later records showed that over a hundred girls of that age were eventually rescued and returned to their parents or sent to domestic situations. 'It was while I was doing this work that I was asked to go to London and see a Mr Stead,' she remembered.[71]

W. T. Stead had first become aware of the existence of white slave traffic in 1876 through Josephine Butler's propaganda. At the time he was, at 25, the turbulent, emotional editor of the influential *Northern Echo*. Acknowledging his support, Mrs Butler wrote: 'I could wish for the sake of justice and virtue that your paper was the most important in the Kingdom. ... In the grandest [brothel] of the kind in Paris, I saw the portraits of all the great men who had frequented them – diplomats, generals and English lords. Oh, it was terrible to see them! The brothel-keepers put a cross underneath the portrait at each visit, to mark the number of visits made to the place by these great men!'

The following year Stead recorded in his diary: 'I want to write a novel on enforced prostitution. I see more clearly than ever its power. ...' By 1880 he was experiencing 'a curious compulsion in the direction of London of a sense of burden which is imposed on me to write an *Uncle Tom's Cabin* on the slavery of England. The burden is greater than I can bear. But if it is ultimately to be laid upon my back, God will strengthen me for it. If I have to write it, I shall have to plunge in the depths of social hell. ...'[72] Five years later Rebecca Jarrett found herself being unwillingly cast as his entrée into that hell.

Benjamin Scott, the gentle, courteous, 75-year-old Chamberlain of the City of London, having assured Bramwell that 'something would be done' appealed to Stead, now editor of the *Pall Mall Gazette*, in an attempt to honour that promise. The House of Commons, 'honeycombed with immorality' as it was, continued to drag the heels of its vested interests in preventing the passing of the Criminal Law Amendment Bill, being obliged to the infamous white slave trader, Mrs Mary[73] Jeffries, meanwhile, for providing Members with circulars advertising 'new attractions'. Not wholly convinced that his hour had come, Stead made other enquiries. Scotland Yard strongly advised him to stay away from the white slave traffic. The Home Secretary banned the police from providing him with any evidence at all. The president of the Council for the Protection of Women and Children indicated that this was a sphere over which they had no control, and the Rev Benjamin Waugh, who had recently founded the NSPCC, introduced him to a four-year-old who had been assaulted by 12 men, only one of whom had been convicted.

Stead's 'sense of burden' led him finally to the office of Bramwell Booth, where, by appointment on Whit Sunday 24 May, he listened to the heart-wrenching stories of several under-16-year-olds, and finally to Rebecca Jarrett herself.[73] 'I was inexorable. I said to her, "You have told me that you have procured and ruined scores of innocent girls. Make amends by procuring one not for ruin, but for rescue, whose purchase will save more girls from being sold in the future."'[74] Feeling utterly dejected, Rebecca could do nothing other than agree.

CHAPTER 12

TO GRAPPLE WITH THE MONSTER AND COME OUT UNHURT

STEAD resolved to set up a Special and Secret Commission of Inquiry to investigate the facts about sexual trafficking which seemed to be overwhelming him from every direction. Spelling out the rationale for this in the *Pall Mall Gazette* of 9 July 1885, he wrote: 'The suggestion that such an inquiry should be undertaken reached the *Pall Mall Gazette* office from ... the City Chamberlain, Mr. Benj. Scott, whose position as chairman of the London Committee for the Prevention of Traffic in English Girls enabled him to speak with considerable authority on this question. He brought news of what is called the Shoreham case – the escape of the girl Annie from a Pimlico brothel, thanks to the address of The Salvation Army on the back of an old hymn book.

'The first step in the inquiry was to ascertain from the headquarters of The Salvation Army whether the story was correctly reported. This brought me into close communication with the chiefs of The Salvation Army, with whom I had previously been in communication on the subject, by whom this inquiry was welcomed with enthusiasm and assisted to the uttermost in every way by all its members from the Chief of the Staff down to the humblest private. And here let me state as a matter of simple justice to The Salvation Army that, so far as our inquiry necessitated operations of rescue, our Commission would have been almost helpless without the aid which was extended to us without stint at any hour of the day or the night, at any sacrifice of personal trouble or risk of personal danger, by the intrepid soldiers of that admirable organization. Nor does that by any means exhaust our indebtedness to the Army. In the elucidation of facts, in the investigation of obscure cases, in the furnishing at a moment's notice of men and women ready to do anything and go anywhere, the aid which we received from Mr. Bramwell Booth and his devoted comrades was simply incalculable, and far exceeding that rendered by all the other existing organizations put together.

'After verifying the facts about the Shoreham case, and being assured of the hearty co-operation and loyal support of the London Committee for the Suppression of the Traffic in English Girls, of Mrs Josephine Butler, whose vast experience was placed unreservedly at our disposal, and of The Salvation Army, the work of investigation was begun in earnest.'

While Bramwell was making arrangements for the Whit weekend appointment with Stead, Florence's diary shows Josephine Butler to have been at Rookwood, quite possibly discussing with Catherine the details of a series of immense meetings which would in a very few weeks inaugurate the Purity Crusade.[77]

On 28 May Florence and the two babies travelled to Blaina – their first visit since Mary's birth – Bramwell having gone to Manchester the night before. Whether he communicated with her by telegram, or whether she wrote her diary entries in retrospect after receiving his letters, Florence recorded on Tuesday 2 June: 'Eliza Armstrong seen by Rebecca at Mrs Broughton's'; the following day: 'Eliza Armstrong bought'; the day after: 'Eliza Armstrong to Paris'; and on Friday 5 June, simply: 'Paris'. Such brevity conceals what Stead called 'the story of an actual pilgrimage into a real hell'.[77]

One of Bramwell's letters to her at Blaina is reproduced in their daughter's biography of him. Dated 11 June, it says: 'This last three weeks I have been wading through a sea of sin and defilement in others. What I have seen, and what I have been compelled to hear has filled me with horror as well as

92

astonishment and pity. It has seemed, many a time, a sin to *think* even of my precious one at all – but my heart when sickened and appalled has turned to you and worshipped, in gratitude to God, the spotless purity and tender love which are yours and yet are mine also. I think I have learned some things out of all this weltering woe; I believe I can see in a way I have not seen it before, that a man and a woman who love God and love each other, can and do glorify Him in the happiness of that very closest union and oneness of flesh as well as spirit.

'I have sometimes had questionings I could not quite answer to myself and have left them: I think I see now – how it is pure love that makes all pure and beautiful and lovely before Him and to each other – and that its absence makes all impure and dark and a gateway to the depths. I say this chiefly because I feel you will have wondered whether this dreadful familiarity with things of which I knew nearly nothing may not have hurt the pureness of mind which you love in me as I love it in you. I think not – I have been *kept*. And you have kept me – my heart and reins and longings are all in your dear hands – and all women are lovable, no matter how defaced and destroyed they may be, because you are a woman and because I have come into your inner heart and treasury and I know you and see the image of God in love and purity of body and soul and spirit. I am sure that without you I could not have gone through this. I don't see how I could – I should have been shaken and torn in pieces and cast down.

'And I see, therefore, one clear good which could come no other way, from the oneness of two who love – in being able to descend into the very pit and look at *that* sin in its nakedness and shamelessness and face it without one single doubt about its supposed necessity, and without one moment's loss of faith in God's plans and arrangements for the world. Without you I could not have answered properly the question, "Is not all this the mere extreme of a necessity of human nature?" You have taught me, and made it possible with the energy of hope linked to the power of experience to grapple with the monster and come out unhurt.

'I have many things to tell you. Some I want to tell you, which, though they will grieve your soul for the sins of the people, yet it will rest my mind to tell you. Many things I must not tell you – you need never, I hope, know all – the world is too dreadful to go on very long – I hope I shall not very greatly burden you with what I feel burdened about; but I think I would like you to know what I know for we are one, and I believe you will believe that I am the same – only that I love you more.'[78]

The focal point of 'all this weltering woe' hinted at in Bramwell's letter may be traced through Florence's four cryptic diary references the preceding week and a series of articles Stead was to publish in the *Pall Mall Gazette* at the beginning of July under the title *The Maiden Tribute of Modern Babylon*. In the first of these, he told the story of a child of 13, bought for £5. He used the pseudonym of 'Lily' to preserve Eliza Armstrong's anonymity.

Devoid of the kind of sensationalism he employed in that exposé, the following account explains his motive for the whole affair: 'I must briefly state what it was that I wished to prove. It was asserted and denied that innocent children could be procured for immoral purposes with the consent of their mothers. It was asserted and denied that a midwife, whose name was given to me, was in the habit of certifying the virginity of young girls before they were dishonoured, that she was willing to undertake their repair after their violation, and, further, that she was willing to sell drugs for the purpose of rendering the children unconscious during the perpetration of the crime. It was also asserted and denied that a brothel-keeper would admit a young girl of thirteen to her premises for immoral purposes, and that she would supply her customers with drink without a licence. And, lastly, it was asserted and denied that girls of thirteen could be taken out of the country, and placed abroad in places where all traces of them could be lost. I wanted to set all these questions at rest once and for all, before committing myself to any statement on the subject.

'On the evening of Derby Day [Wednesday 3 June], I went by appointment to Albany Street and had tea with Eliza Armstrong and Mrs [Rebecca] Jarrett. The conversation was general, and I need hardly say that I was most careful to say nothing that could in any way lead the child to suspect the purpose for which she had been procured. After she had left the room, Mrs Jarrett told me how she had got the girl. She said she had paid £2 to the procuress and £1 to the mother. £2 more was to be sent to the former if the child was all right – that is to say, if she was found to be pure. If she was not pure, she had to be returned as she went – that is to say, without being tampered with by any man, and no more money was to be paid. I asked Mrs Jarrett if she was quite sure the mother consented, knowing why her daughter was wanted. "Quite sure," she replied. Jarrett told me distinctly that she had told the mother her daughter was wanted for a man and she must be pure.

'I had only known Jarrett about a week, but she came to me with an emphatic testimonial as to her trustworthiness. So far as I could see, there was no reason to distrust her. She had not volunteered for this work. I had thrust her into it, she being most unwilling. Her consent had been wrung from her by an appeal to her sense of her own guilt in the past, and her desire to make reparation in the future. She had broken with her old friends and her prospects would be ruined if she played me false. Having thus, through a trusty agent, bought Eliza Armstrong, I determined to make her the unconscious instrument of checking such sales in the future.

'First of all there was the midwife. I sent … my courier to explain that a wealthy gentleman, with a penchant for little children, had procured a little girl of whose virginity he wished to be satisfied before seduction. Would she examine the child for that purpose? The midwife made no objection and an appointment was made for the Wednesday evening. Her fee for the purpose was one guinea. Rebecca Jarrett and [my courier] attended with the girl Eliza at the hour fixed. The child was told that it was necessary to see that she was all right for her situation, and she consented. The examination was momentary, and no objection whatever was made by the girl. The midwife sold [my courier] a bottle of chloroform, a small bottle for which he paid thirty shillings. Its value at a chemist's would be about one shilling.

'I met the party outside the door and accompanied them to Poland Street. The woman who kept the house of accommodation above the ham-and-beef shop made no difficulty about giving us accommodation. It was a little before ten o'clock, and the child thought she had come to a hotel. We took two rooms for the four of us, paying about seven and sixpence a room. In order that there might be no doubt as to the knowledge of the keeper of the house of the youth of the child, we summoned her upstairs and ordered some whisky and lemonade. She brought us the spirit, which we threw away when her back was turned, and drank the lemonade. In order to make quite sure that the child could be procured and placed quite at my mercy in a brothel, I asked Jarrett to call me in. … Emptying a little chloroform on a handkerchief, Jarrett asked the child to take a good sniff of it. The child, not liking the smell, flung the handkerchief away. …The administering of the drug … was with no intent to do her harm. It was to shield her from knowing even that a man had entered her room, that she was asked to sniff the handkerchief. I wished her to be kept quite ignorant of the whole affair. I wanted her to be sound asleep when I entered her room, and it was not until Jarrett assured me she was sleeping that I entered the room. Unfortunately she was not asleep. My step – for I never spoke – roused her. She cried out, as many another poor child has done in London brothels, "There is a man in the room." I at once withdrew. Mrs Jarrett soothed the child, and told her it would be better to go elsewhere for a quieter lodging. She dressed her and took her to a respectable house, where she passed the night.'[79]

Here Bramwell takes up the story and it becomes clear to whom that 'respectable house' belonged: 'It was important … to have it certified after this experience, that nothing had happened to the child, and accordingly it was agreed that she should be taken from the brothel … straight to the house of a specialist whose name I had suggested, and who had most warmly agreed to help us, and that the specialist, after examining her, should furnish a certificate.'[80] That specialist was Dr Heywood Smith, of the Lying-in Hospital.[81]

'Next morning', continued Stead, 'I sent her to Paris. I had two reasons for doing this. First, I wished to show the ease with which a girl who had been ruined might be made to disappear abroad, and secondly I wished to place her as far as possible from the influence of a drunken mother, who had sold her child to shame. ... In order to secure that the girl should be placed in good hands at a distance from home, I applied to Mr Bramwell Booth for help in this matter. Mr Booth responded to my request with the readiness which the chiefs of The Salvation Army have ever shown when an opportunity was offered them of doing anything, however slight, to seek and save the fallen and the lost. ... I undertook to pay all expenses, including the child's wages, while she was being trained to household work in the situation which was found for her in France, if he, on the other hand, would see that she was well done to, carefully trained and brought up in a Christian home. He consented. ...'

At Charing Cross Station on Thursday morning 4 June, Bramwell received Eliza from Rebecca, and Elizabeth Combe, a French-Swiss Salvation Army officer, took her safely to Paris.[81]

Eleven days later Florence returned from Blaina in time to join in the public celebrations of the 30th anniversary of 'the General's wedding' at the Great Western Hall, Marylebone, the following day. (An echo here of the failure to mention the bride in announcements of her own wedding three years earlier.) Her diary records: 'Monday June 15, 1885: Travelled home, arriving Paddington 5.45. So delightful to see my darling one, though he looks very worn. It is a hard cross to glory in, this seeing him daily killed. Called in at Rookwood on our way, just to show the babies. General looking very weary and voice hoarse, having just returned from meetings in the country. Heard Bailey had been very poorly.'

For some months there had been talk of moving house. On 17 June 'Went down to see the new house with Mr Eason. No paper up yet or paint.' The following day she went to see 'poor Mrs Crick' (her midwife), the doctor having said 'it is impossible for her to recover'. With Florence's babies arriving at two-yearly intervals over the next 10 years this could have presented a difficulty. Perhaps there was more to the inauguration of Salvation Army maternity work a few months later than meets the eye! On Friday 19 June she was welcomed back to the refuge after her 'maternity leave':

'Miss S and the officers had a very bright welcome for me, and Esther Walker had worked upon pieces of red stuff "Welcome Home", "God bless the Chief and his wife", "Our love to Mrs Bramwell and Miss Sapsworth". ... Went to Holiness Meeting in the evening led by the General. B gone to Stead and not home till 11.30.

'Saturday June 20, 1885: Worked hard all day packing ready to move. ... Bramwell not home to dinner – has not been once since I returned yet. Said he would come at 8 but did not arrive until [blank]. Feel he cannot go on at this long. I must keep him on the altar and trust in God. ...Went over in the evening to see the house with Mr Eason. We shall manage to make the carpets fit both rooms. The papers are very pretty.

'Monday June 22, 1885: Moved into our new house at 89 Darenth Road' (less than half a mile away, at the other side of Clapton Common). 'Very busy to pack up as, being Sunday, things were not in good order, also I am a novice at this and there was no one to help us. Bailey and Hicks worked well. There was more furniture than Mr Eason reckoned for, and at least 3 more loads, so we did not get done till 11pm. We were all dead tired.

'Tuesday June 23, 1885: In the midst of putting the house straight came telegram from Mrs Butler asking me to go to Winchester as poor Rebecca was much discouraged and upset, wanting to give up the work and return to London. We wired and wrote, deciding to go tomorrow.

'Wednesday June 24, 1885: Went down to Winchester by 2:15 train, taking the little baby and Alice [the Training Home] nurse. Rebecca met us at the station. We drove to Mrs Butler's, who was out and then on to Rebecca's cottage and had tea with her 5 rescue girls – or rather I had tea with Rebecca alone and had nice talk and prayer. She had in great measure gained the victory that morning.

'Thursday June 25, 1885: …Went to dinner with Rebecca and her girls. Had two minutes prayer afterwards. Then went visiting in the worst street of the town with Rebecca. Got into one brothel where the keeper had been ill. Had talk with her and three girls and prayer. The old woman went on her knees for the first time in her life she said. Promised to go and see Rebecca. …

'Went to take tea at the Home of Rest. Eager welcome from Rhoda and Amelia. A poor little thing of 13 is here expecting to be confined. Oh the terrible consequences of this sin upon us, while the men are scot-free. Oh God how long!! … The bus did not call for us and we missed the train. Had to wait until 7.40, not getting home until 11. B came home just after us. He is working infinitely hard and will knock up. It is a trial to me to give him up to this. My beautiful pure angel – He can never be the same quite.

'Friday June 26, 1885: Was going to the meeting but Mama came in just as I was washing baby to go and said I was too knocked up, which I was.

'Thursday July 2, 1885: … Had prayer meeting with the officers and Miss S. Read the last few verses in Jude. Had not much liberty as Miss S immediately picked up the question as to whether we should go on forgiving the bad girls etc. Oh God give me wisdom and strength to carry out what I feel to be right. Came home at 4. Dear baby been so good. Rested an hour, had tea, went to R to see dear Mama who is ill. Saw Baroness de Gingin from Switzerland.

'Friday July 3, 1885: …I went over to write for Mama who is very ill with dysentery. Put down the stair carpet – a very awkward job. … B very late doing Stead's business with Vint and reading proofs of what is to appear on Monday.'

On Saturday 4 July Stead published a 'Notice to Our Readers: A Frank Warning' which in part read: 'The Criminal Law Amendment Bill … has thrice been passed through the House of Lords, and now for the third time it is threatened with extinction in the House of Commons. The public, it is said, is not interested in the subject, and the bill, therefore, may safely be abandoned. That we are told is the calculation in high quarters. But if Ministers think of allowing the bill to drop because the public is not keenly alive to its importance, it is necessary to open the eyes of the public, in order that a measure, the urgency of which has been repeatedly admitted, may pass into law this session. We have, therefore, determined, with a full sense of the responsibility attaching to such a decision, to publish the report of a Special and Secret Commission of Inquiry which we appointed to examine into the whole subject. It is a long, detailed report, dealing with those phases of sexual criminality which the Criminal Law Amendment Bill was framed to repress. Nothing but the most imperious sense of public duty would justify its publication. But as we are assured on every hand, on the best authority, that without its publication the bill will be abandoned for the third time, we dare not face the responsibility of its suppression. We shall, therefore, begin its publication on Monday, and continue to publish … until the whole infernal narrative is complete.

'But although we are thus compelled, in the public interest, to publish the case for the bill, or rather for those portions of it which are universally admitted to be necessary, we have no desire to inflict upon unwilling eyes the ghastly story of the criminal developments of modern vice. Therefore we say quite frankly today that all those who are squeamish, and all those who are prudish, and all those who prefer to live in a fool's paradise of imaginary innocence and purity, selfishly oblivious to the horrible realities which torment those whose lives are passed in the London Inferno, will do well not to read the *Pall Mall Gazette* of Monday and the three following days. The story of an actual pilgrimage into a real hell is not pleasant reading, and is not meant to be. It is, however, an authentic record of unimpeachable facts, "abominable, unutterable, and worse than fables yet have feigned or fear conceived". But it is true, and its publication is necessary.'

Against this backdrop was celebrated the 20th anniversary of The Salvation Army, and Florence was there: 'Sunday July 5, 1885:

Anniversary of the SA. I marched down with the General and corps to Congress Hall, stayed morning meeting and walked up again. G talked splendidly upon "There is therefore now no condemnation to those who walk" etc. ...'

It was a text whose truth was soon to be tested. The pages Bramwell had been proof-reading late into the night on Friday appeared in Monday's edition of the *Pall Mall Gazette* as the first instalment of *The Maiden Tribute of Modern Babylon*. A lengthy introduction explained the classical roots of the title, which, in essence, and heavily précised, read: 'In ancient times ... Athens, after a disastrous campaign, was compelled by her conqueror to send once every nine years a tribute to Crete of seven youths and seven maidens ... who ... returned no more. The vessel that bore them to Crete unfurled black sails as the symbol of despair, and on arrival her passengers were flung into the ... Labyrinth ... there to wander about blindly until such time as they were devoured by the Minotaur, a frightful monster, half man, half bull, the foul product of an unnatural lust. ...

'This very night in London, and every night, year in and year out, not seven maidens only, but many times seven ... will be offered up as *the Maiden Tribute of Modern Babylon*. Maidens they were when this morning dawned, but tonight their ruin will be accomplished, and tomorrow they will find themselves within the portals of the maze of London brotheldom. Within that labyrinth wander, like lost souls, the vast host of London prostitutes, whose numbers no man can compute, but who are probably not much below 50,000 strong. ... The maw of the London Minotaur is insatiable, and none that go into the secret recesses of his lair return again ... most of those ensnared tonight will perish, some of them in horrible torture. ... London's lust annually uses up many thousands of women, who are literally killed and made away with – living sacrifices in the service of vice.

'That may be inevitable, and with that I have nothing to do. But I do ask that those doomed to the house of evil fame shall not be trapped into it unwillingly, and that none shall be beguiled into the chamber of death before they are of an age to read the inscription above the portal – "All hope abandon ye who enter here." If the daughters of the people must be served up as dainty morsels to minister to the passions of the rich, let them at least attain an age when they can understand the nature of the sacrifice which they are asked to make. And if we must cast maidens – not seven, but seven times seven – nightly into the jaws of vice, let us at least see to it that they assent to their own immolation, and are not unwilling sacrifices procured by force and fraud. …'

As this scandal hit the streets of London, down at 89 Darenth Road domestic issues were following their Monday morning course: 'Monday July 6, 1885: Housework in the morning, linen etc, and washed pocket-handkerchiefs until the skin came off [my fingers]. Went to auxiliary meeting at Congress [Hall] in afternoon. Saw Mrs Butler's niece. … Talk all about the devilish revelations of London. My whole heart is sick. Seems as if it took all the brightness out of everything. Did not get home until 9. B stayed to the All Night [of Prayer]. I sent the two servants. Found Mr Metcalf here with a sad story of a child, 14, in trouble through her brother.'

The following morning scores of City newsboys were arrested for selling the prurient paper (the Lord Mayor later dismissing the summons) while Northumberland Street, where the paper's offices were, was blocked with men and boys literally fighting to get hold of a copy. The young George Bernard Shaw, a reviewer for the paper, took a bundle out into the Strand and sold them himself.[87]

After refuge work in the morning of Wednesday 8 July, the day the third part of the exposé appeared, 'Went on to 101 to speak to Bramwell. Found him just going somewhere on the "devilish business" and not able to speak to me. Got home about 3.30. Too dead tired to eat anything. …'

CHAPTER 13

IF WE WIN, WE WIN, AND IF WE LOSE, WE WIN

HAVING 'never felt so proud of [Bramwell] in my life,'[82] Catherine Booth now plunged herself into the series of great meetings nationwide inaugurating the Purity Crusade. The entries in her daughter-in-law's diary are full of it:

'Monday July 13, 1885: Prince's Hall Meeting for Ladies only.

'Tuesday July 14, 1885: Prince's Hall Meeting. Samuel Morley [MP] in the chair. Lord Mount Temple, Samuel Smith etc.

'Thursday July 16, 1885: Mass Meeting in Exeter Hall. A.1.

'Wednesday July 22, 1885: Woman's Meeting Exeter Hall. Splendid. Body of Hall nearly full. Mrs Booth A.1. Two little ruined girls 13 and 15 brought on to platform.

'General at Albert Hall, Sheffield.'

In *The War Cry* of that date he was reported as having told a huge and excited crowd at the Congress Hall, 'I should like us to go on thundering and lightning until the atmosphere is cleared ... but one voice at least shall speak, *the voice of The Salvation Army!* We are asking the Government tonight to protect, to put a guard, a hedge, round young and ignorant girls. ... We must let the Houses of Parliament know that when we got the light it was given to people not afraid to hold up the torch.'

Florence's own attempts 'to put a guard, a hedge, round young and ignorant girls' continued unabated:

'Thursday July 23, 1885: Have been tremendously busy this week and last. Impossible to keep diary written up. Today went to refuge. Found Miss Sapsworth in one of her down fits of disturbance – very trying. Annie Lucas possessed of the Devil. Mrs Reynolds there with the little ruined Lizzie. Obliged to stop. ...

'Sunday July 26, 1885: Holiness Meeting at Stoke Newington 10.45. Have undertaken these morning meetings for a while. Mrs Onslow came down with me. Mrs Bulman was there. Had a pretty good meeting.

'Tuesday July 28, 1885: Large Meeting Congress Hall. General, Mama, Professor Stuart M.P.'

Somewhere in the preceding week little Catherine's second birthday passed unrecorded in her mother's diary, though she did note on Friday 31 July that 'Balls [the Salvationist cabman][85] brought a little dog for Catherine'. It was to be the first of many much-loved little dogs she and her sisters were to companion with into extreme old age. Meanwhile, her Grandmama Catherine was addressing letters to such national figures as Queen Victoria and Prime Ministers Gladstone and Salisbury successively, more than once declaring that if the Criminal Law Amendment Bill were not passed, she would 'turn away from the fathers to the mothers ... and would march at the head of 50,000 mothers to Buckingham Palace to petition the Queen, The Mother of the Nation.'[83]

That, however, proved not to be necessary, for in response to a petition printed in the 18 July *War Cry*, 393,000 signatures were received in only 17 days, made into a gigantic roll and on Thursday 30 July drawn on a dray to Westminster by four white horses, headed by a brass band and accompanied by hundreds of marching Salvationists.[84]

All the rescue girls went into Epping Forest on Wednesday 5 August, not on a dray, but in a 'brake'. This was so that the contents of the refuge could be moved from Hanbury Street to 48 Navarino Road, Dalston.

'Tuesday August 11, 1885: Such a rush. No time for diary. 101 [Queen Victoria Street] in morning. ... WBB [Bramwell] at Rookwood till past 11. HBB [Bramwell's brother Herbert] in for a bath.'

On Sunday 9 August Florence had expressed 'Great Anxiety about R.J.', which intensified by Wednesday 12 August: 'A long day at the refuge today. Rebecca went yesterday down to Mrs Reynolds and saw *St James' Gazette*, so was rather upset thereat. Wanted to start off to Colchester alone last night. Felt better after a good talk with me. Still, she would be happier with Captain Jones' (her original Northampton saviour, now stationed at Colchester) 'until her cottage is ready, so we sent her off. Mama came down to see her. ...

'Thursday August 13, 1885: A woman's meeting at Congress Hall at night. Curtain [partition] down, but quite full. One of Mama's stirring addresses. Refuge girls all there. ...'

The Criminal Law Amendment Act finally passed into law by a large majority on 14 August, without diary comment by Florence, despite the fact that the whole affair had been precipitated originally by her own horrendous disclosures. The immediate main effects were that:

It raised the age of consent from 13 to 16 years of age;

It made it a criminal offence to procure girls for prostitution by administering drugs, intimidation or fraud;

It punished householders who permitted under-age sex on their premises;

It made it a criminal offence to abduct a girl under 18 without her consent for purposes of carnal knowledge;

It gave magistrates the power to issue search warrants to find missing females;

It gave power to the court to remove a girl from her legal guardians if they condoned her seduction;

It provided for summary proceedings to be taken against brothels; and

It raised the age of felonious assaults to 13 and misdemeanor assault between 13 and 16 as well as imbecile women and girls.[86]

Any rejoicing this may have subsequently caused Mrs Bramwell's household was brought to an abrupt halt on Saturday 29 August. The following day she disclosed: 'Sunday August 30,

1885: Bad news about Rebecca. Detectives came to see B on Saturday asking where she was. He did not tell me till this morning as thought it would worry me. He is very much worried about it indeed. R came up from Colchester last night with Archer. Her case put in the hands of Shepherd Allen. Took Holiness Meeting at Stoke Newington as usual. Spoke on the work of the Holy Spirit and read Romans 8: "There is therefore now ..."

'Went to see R at Miss Sapsworth's at 8 o'clock, but found she was very down and not inclined to come, so walked on to Aspland Road (Archer's) where she was – found her in bed asleep, but awoke her and had a cheer up talk. Gave her "Counted worthy to suffer for Jesus' sake" as a pillow. Came back very tired indeed. B very poorly.

'Wednesday September 2, 1885: R before magistrate, Mr Poland public prosecutor etc. I went to Navarino Road as usual. Did good morning's work. Was upstairs after dinner with Mrs Hill when Eva [Bramwell's sister] came over to tell me of the news of the summons against Bramwell, Mr Stead and Madame Combe. Felt it very much because B seems so worried, but I must trust in God. Miss Humbert and Hawker [Captain Jones] were looking after Rebecca. Tried to get her some food in, but not understanding it was only at 12 o'clock, were too late.

'Saw Rebecca, who had a good cry, poor thing. The lies and the being called "that woman" she felt so much. She was in a most disagreeable stinking hole – a very small cell with just a bench round; a very bad smell. She could only be seen and spoken to through a small square grating, and opposite to hers were other similar ones. A low looking man [the gaoler[1]] could look at them all the time.

'Thursday September 3, 1885: To 48 Navarino Road this morning and then on to Clerkenwell 12:30 to see Rebecca with Archer, Miss Humbert and Jones. Called at Headquarters and Mr Reed of Romford was kind enough to accompany us. We arrived at the gaol and found our way to a small door in the great high wall where stood about a dozen people and a tall policeman. The people had, like us, come to see prisoners. We were only allowed in four at a time and the first four returned before the next four were admitted. Only one visitor to each prisoner is the rule, but Mr Reed, who stood with us, asked to see the deputy governor and came back with permission for Miss Humbert (a co-worker with Mrs Butler) to accompany me.'

Florence's next diary entry being Saturday 12 September – the scene with which this story commenced – we do well to question why Rebecca had been thrown into prison early in September, and how it came about that Florence was spending her 24th birthday in Bow Street Police Court, with Bramwell in the dock.

Two months earlier, on 13 July, *The Pall Mall Gazette* had picked up on a report carried the day before by its rival, *Lloyd's Weekly Newspaper*, about 'a poor but apparently respectable woman' appearing at Marylebone police court to renew an application to the magistrate for advice in regard to her daughter, whom, she said, she had not seen or heard of since last May. A neighbour had asked if she would like her daughter to go out to service, and that if she did she knew of a very nice situation. The girl was spoken to, and after some consultation the applicant was persuaded to consent to the girl going to the place, which was said to be at Croydon, the only condition being that she should write home to her parents once a week. She left home to go to the lady at Croydon on Derby Day, and had not been heard of since. Her neighbour had received a sovereign and a letter from the girl's mistress stating that her daughter was quite well, but when the mother wrote to her daughter at the address given, which was near Manchester, the letter was returned by the Post Office as 'not known'. The woman said her girl was only 13 years of age, and after having read what had recently been published in an evening newspaper she greatly feared some harm had overtaken her daughter.

The magistrate asked: 'Do you mean to say that you let the girl go away with strangers without having made further inquiry than what you have just explained?'

Applicant: 'Well, sir, she said I should hear from her every week.'

Magistrate: 'Then I consider it very great negligence on your part. You know you are the mother of the girl, and she is under age.'

By direction of the magistrate inquiry was made into the matter, and it was subsequently reported that the woman who had the girl had been at one time a fellow servant of the applicant's neighbour. The reason for the letter being returned by the Post Office was that it had been addressed to a place near Manchester instead of near Winchester. The magistrate directed that the matter should be inquired into further.

The woman applying to the magistrate for advice was, of course, Mrs Armstrong, who, egged-on by neighbours, had put two-and-two together as far as 'Lily' and Eliza were concerned and was determined not to be seen as the drunken mother who had sold her daughter for immoral purposes, as reported by Stead. 'The lady at Croydon' to whom Eliza supposedly went was, of course, Rebecca, and it was to Rebecca's Winchester refuge that the further enquiries ordered by the magistrate led. Rebecca not being there, they were directed to Bramwell Booth back in London.

'The police told me they had been searching for me in every place they could think of,' Rebecca remembered, 'so I told them I was ready and willing to go with them. We had a lovely prayer meeting first. Several people prayed for me. I opened my dear old Bible, given to me by Mrs [Josephine] Butler, at the 42nd chapter of Isaiah, and then I began to shout with joy. The police ran upstairs and I showed them the message what my Father had sent me to give me strength. That night I went to Bow Street and gave myself up. The lawyer and some of my friends went with me to see me safe into Bow Street. I was put into a cell, but they were all very kind to me directly they found out I was quiet. In fact, one of the police brought me a cushion for my head, so I felt a good deal better. ...

'Well, the next morning I had some food sent in from outside, and then I was taken to the [police] station and charged with taking a young girl without the father's consent. The fact is I never saw the father; it was the mother who handed over the girl to me. The whole trouble was poor Mr Stead's paper coming out in such blazing large letters at night. The S.A. had nothing to do with it; they let Mr Stead have me as a poor tool to show up all the wrong which was being done. The dear old Army clung to me to keep me right.'[88] Chief among those clingers was 24-year-old Mrs Bramwell.

On Monday 7 September, Stead, Bramwell, Rebecca, Elizabeth Combe, Jacques (Stead's courier) and Madame Mourez (the examining midwife) appeared in Bow Street police court, charged with 'taking and causing to be taken one Eliza Armstrong, an unmarried girl under the age of 16, out of the possession and against the will of Charles Armstrong, her father, and Elizabeth Armstrong, her mother;' with 'unlawfully and feloniously taking away and detaining Eliza Armstrong, a child under the age of 14, with intent to deprive her parents of the possession of such child;' with conspiring together to commit this offence; with administering and causing to be administered 'a certain noxious thing' to Eliza Armstrong; and with committing an indecent assault on her.[89]

The case lasted 19 days – six days of committal proceedings before the Bow Street magistrate, followed some weeks later by a 13-day trial by judge and jury at the Central Criminal Court – the Old Bailey.[91]

'Every blackguard in London must have assembled in Bow Street while the case was before the magistrate,' remembered Bramwell. 'From every foul den in the metropolis the people had come to gloat on the discomfiture of these modern Galahads. I was mobbed more than once, dragged out of a cab, and maltreated, and only rescued with difficulty by a police inspector, who drove the crowd right and left. On more than one occasion the police placed a "Black Maria" at our disposal, and we were rapidly conveyed from the Court to some distant Square, where cabs could be available for us. And, apart from the mob who shook *our* heads, there were the righteous and respectable people who shook their own. They were agreed as to the evil, were, in fact, horrified that such things could be in their midst, but, with here and there an exception, they strongly disapproved our methods of meeting it. It was impossible to disapprove of theirs, because they gave no hint of having any.'[90]

The committal proceedings having, in the view of the magistrate, proved there was a case to answer, what had become known as the Armstrong Affair would in the fullness of time be played out in the presence of judge and jury at the Central Criminal Court.[91] Meanwhile the prisoners were released on bail.

In the weeks before the Old Bailey trial began, 'the Army went on growing at a pace embarrassing to its leaders, yet never quickly enough to satisfy them',[92] notwithstanding the fact that because of the Armstrong case any wearer of its uniform was the subject of the vilest insults and often assaults. At 89 Darenth Road, Commissioner and Mrs Railton with their two children came for a weekend; the following week, Frederick de Latour Tucker. Pioneer of the Army's expansion to India in 1882, he would eventually marry Bramwell's sister Emma, but was on this occasion at IHQ to consult with other Army leaders. 'Major Tucker came to sleep,' records his future sister-in-law. 'Cath so amused – said "funny man, all toes".' One glance at the photograph taken at Mr Eason's studio on 6 October, and the two-year-old's remark becomes clear: Major Tucker habitually wore Indian garb, as on this occasion did little Cath. At the end of that day Florence confided to her diary that she had 'made many resolutions. Felt rather poorly – cold.' No surprise there. Besides a stream of notable house guests, her work at the refuge continued full pelt – not to mention her corps ministry.

'Sunday October 4, 1885: Holiness meeting at Stoke Newington. Walked down alone. Hard time at first, but a brake [sic] in the prayer meeting – 1 man, 2 refuge girls and 1 man for salvation. Walked home alone. Commissioner and Mrs Railton up all day to consult with Tucker and Commissioner Smith. I wrote letters and piece for *The Christian*. Felt very tired and burdened. Refuge a great anxiety – all rescue people seem so unbelieving. Mama at Rink – "Not this man but Barabbas".

'Wednesday October 7, 1885: To refuge at 9:30. Spent most time at 46. ... Spoke to girls in workroom about supporting the officers in *their* efforts to help *them*. Went on to Roses – bought Cath's winter jacket. Went on to Congress [Hall]. ... Did not get home till 4. Found B had arrived. In a few minutes Madam Moreau and Abel arrived. Had dinner altogether – short commons, as rather unexpected. ...

'Thursday October 8, 1885: To see Miss Wells with Cath first. Officers' meeting and farewell to Commissioner Smith at Congress Hall. ... Meeting lasted till 1:30. Good, but nothing unusual. ... Drove to refuge ... Home and wrote letters. Cut out Cath's winter coat. EMB and HHB home with COS [Bramwell] at 6. ... General made disturbance about their working so hard. B and Tucker sat up late talking.'

The following three days her cold was so bad she stayed home. Bramwell, in spite of seeming to Florence 'still very down and poorly', worked on, as usual, throughout the weekend. Her sister Evie arrived on Saturday afternoon and 'took Cath for a walk in her new thick coat'. In the evening they 'drowned the black mouse with a swelling'. (Little Catherine's earliest memory of her father would be of when he lifted her up to peer into a nest of white mice, perhaps a year later.[93] They seem to have had more success with them than with the swollen one!)

'Sunday October 11, 1885: Asked Mrs Onslow to take my meeting on account of my cold. Dearest spent the morning at Rookwood. Evie and I saw to the babies and had a time of reading and writing. Read Mrs Fletcher and was much struck about her resolutions of getting up in the morning in spite of weakness of body. Also she speaks of curbing her appetite. Feel I can rejoice in victory over the *world* and the *devil* – but the flesh needs more attention. Wrote several letters to my girls. Had nice time of prayer with Evie in the evening. In the afternoon she took Cath for a walk while I rested. Herbert came in the afternoon. B, Herbert and Cath went to Rookwood to tea and B stayed until 10.30. Babs poorly with a cold. Took fresh courage.

'Monday October 12, 1885: Refuge in open trap. Took Evie and Cath. Cath to [Training Home], whence she came back by a cadet. Saw and dismissed Mary Cook – about the worst girl I have ever known or heard of. So utterly hardened. No truth in her. ... Went to rest. B came home meantime and I was not up to greet him. This our wedding [anniversary]. ... Toothache. Interesting talk about sacraments and India after dinner. Made wool bonnet for Mary, who is still very poorly.

'Tuesday October 13, 1885: Refuge in the morning. Wilfred called with Miss Berry. Left her with me. I could get nothing out of her. Went round with them to see their little house. Had a little prayer. Home. ... Staff meeting at Congress Hall in the evening. I got a blessing, but the meeting was rather stiff, the shadow of recent traitorous resignations being over us all. Major Tucker spoke, my precious B led – rambled on in his style that I like, from faith to love – then love to faith.

'Wednesday October 14, 1885: Wilfred's wedding. Took Cath down. She was frightened at the noise at first, but afterwards clapped her hands and sang. She must come to a few more meetings. ... Saw Brandt, who has written to Emma saying she wants to come and nurse my little ones. This seems to be of the Lord. Cath's being at the meeting so made her heart go out towards her that she wrote the note at once. Oh, I pray that this may be of the Lord! Major [Oliphant], EMB, CCB, HHB in to spend the evening. Great talk. Dr Metcalf called. Poor Mama suffering greatly with bad ears. God is leading us on to victory.'

Florence was at a 'most enthusiastic gathering' at Exeter Hall the following evening, one of many being held up and down the country during those weeks. Stead and Josephine Butler were among the speakers. The next day 'Dear Rebecca told me it was well with her soul. She had had good times with the Lord. He had revealed to her that she might have to go to prison and that if so the wicked Mrs Jeffries should also be punished.' Was this meeting with Rebecca the cause of Florence's 'dreadful nightmare' that night, waking from which she 'actually rang the servants up'? 'Felt dreadfully tired' the next morning, but better that evening, 'and very happy in God'.

The Grand Jury being charged on Monday 19 October was a significant enough occasion for the General to preside that evening over a Half Night of Prayer at Clapton Congress Hall. He stirred his soldiers by declaring, 'If we win, we win, and if we lose, we win.'[94] It would be a long three weeks before the Army would be in a position not only to calculate its 'winnings', but also to lick its wounds.

CHAPTER 14

THEY BROUGHT WITH THEM KNITTING NEEDLES AND YARN

THE Old Bailey trial commenced on Friday 23 October, necessitating more houseguests at Darenth Road – Dr Washington Ranger, the Army's solicitor, and Major Mrs Caroline Reynolds, who had been deeply involved in Stead's Secret Commission of Inquiry. Proceedings continued on Saturday, but even on Sunday, having had responsibility for the Stoke Newington meeting in the morning, Florence 'Got no rest at all – men in all day. Gave statement re Jarrett to Dr Ranger, afternoon.' Girls and staff from the refuge were coming and going meanwhile, and Bailey had to be talked to about Brandt. Nevertheless, 'Felt need of being more humble in my own soul,' she found time to record.

On Tuesday 27 October, 'Dr Heywood Smith's evidence was very painfully given. He was most embarrassed, dear fellow, and unfortunately let it be only too apparent, and certainly made it seem worse for Bramwell than any amount of open confession. Still, God knows there is nothing to be ashamed of and I trust no one will be cruel enough to injure Dr Smith.' Cruel enough they were. When his part in the proceedings became known, Dr Smith lost his position at the Lying-in Hospital and was subsequently subjected to persecution.[81]

By Thursday 29 October, 'If we do triumph it will indeed be against long odds. Circumstances seem in one way to have conspired against us, and yet it is a farce, the prosecution.' Even so, Florence 'felt the presence of God and think the "bitterness of

115

death" with regard to their going to prison was passed through this morning. My whole soul afterwards seemed just swallowed up with the desire to be better, more after God's pattern.' The following day: 'Would that God could lay our hearts open before the judge and jury – it seems so impossible to get the truth out when everyone is interested in misrepresenting us and will drag the precious Army down if they possibly can. ...'

On Tuesday 3 November, 'Bramwell went into the box after lunch and God wonderfully supported him.' Elsewhere Florence recorded, 'My dear one's partial deafness made his cross-examination an ordeal for me as I could not be near him to help.[95] ... The attorney began nastily but found he could not bully this witness. There was not the slightest hitch or misrepresentation on any point. ...' Later Madame Combe was 'put into the box' and 'the judge said, "I wonder what the case is against Madame Combe?" Attorney had to say, "Well my Lord, eh ..." and Madame was discharged.' Afterwards, Florence 'went with B to Exeter Hall where he and Combe had a splendid shout' (good early Army jargon, this, meaning not that Bramwell and the dear Swiss officer were themselves shouting, but that the congregation cheered at their appearing). 'Training Homes had been blazing away all day there' (again, not to be taken literally, but that the cadets were full of enthusiasm). 'B and I left before the meeting was over and drove home in a handsome (sic) [hansom cab]. Very pleasant time together. I love him more and more.'

After the usual detailed record of the trial proceedings on Thursday 5 November, Florence 'felt a little down about home affairs – have been so much away and life such a rush – but must go on. How much happier I am to belong to those in the dock than any others in that court.'

The judge commenced his summing-up on Saturday 7 November, taking some five hours. Not until 3.40 did the jury retire. Press coverage indicated that relatives and friends of the defendants were there in force – Mrs Stead, Josephine Butler, Florence Booth wearing a Salvation Army bonnet, and a sizeable contingent of other ladies 'attired in the distinctive habit of General Booth's organisation'. 'For these persons', said the *Telegraph*, 'the proceedings must have had an absorbing interest; but careful not to waste the passing time, they had brought with them knitting needles and yarn'[96] – shades not only of Madame Defarge, but of that other 'Important New Departure' Florence would pioneer early in the next century.

Bramwell, also careful not to waste the passing time, wrote letters with his quill pen while the jury were out. This to his wife, sitting elsewhere in the court:

'... I have yours and it has done me good. Of course I cannot hear the judge, but I know from Stead what he is saying. Very bad for us all. I can only stay my soul on God and hope in *Him*. Stead says he feels sure he and Jarrett will be convicted, and I suppose that humanly speaking that looks likely. But then have we not left it all to the Lord – will He not do what is best?

'I fancy the judge has made a great impression against us on the jury. It is therefore quite possible we may be found guilty, and in that case I should be sentenced at once, I believe. However, I am not in bad spirits. I do not think Stead is. If we have to suffer we will. God keep you, my own love, in safety and confidence and joy. Ever yours only, for ever.'

And later: 'Another line, while we are waiting for the coming of the jury. I love you more than ever I did in my life – your whole-hearted bravery in this thing all through has been more to me than words can tell. Keep believing.'[97]

With the reappearance of the jury after three hours' deliberation came the verdicts: Bramwell and Jacques were found not guilty of taking Eliza Armstrong out of the possession of her father against his will, but a verdict of guilty was returned against Rebecca Jarrett and Stead. Three days later a second, shorter, trial was convened to determine whether Stead, Rebecca, Jacques and Madame Mourez were guilty of indecent assault against Eliza. The jury found all four guilty. Stead was sentenced to be 'imprisoned without hard labour for three calendar months', Rebecca to be 'imprisoned without hard labour for six calendar months', Jacques for one month, and Madame Mourez, the professional abortionist, to be 'imprisoned and kept to hard labour for six calendar months'.[96] Florence observed, 'Madame Mourez, poor old thing, was a pitiable sight all day.' The hard labour was to prove too much for her. She died in prison.

'Rebecca was in very good spirits', according to Florence, 'and will be blessed in going to prison, I am sure.' And so it proved. 'Mrs Bramwell' did all she could to lighten Rebecca's imprisonment, writing to her whenever permitted[95] and visiting Millbank prison on Tuesday 22 December. 'Saw Mr Merrick, the chaplain. Found R reported as well and happy and after 18 January she can be visited once – four people at a time – and can receive letters. Madame Mourez is said to be dangerously ill. God have mercy on her soul – unless indeed she has become too given over to hideous wickedness, a monster in human form, which seems most probable. We must try and visit her too.' On the diary page for Saturday 17 April Florence had noted in advance: 'Rebecca comes out of jail.' On the actual day, she recorded: 'Went at 7 this morning with Miss Asdell who came up in the trap to see R out. So thankful and relieved to find her in splendid spirits and am convinced that she is much improved.'

When Rebecca died 'full of years and piety' in 1928 at the age of 81, it was the baby Catherine Booth, firstborn of Bramwell and Florence and by then the leader of the Women's Social Work in her own right, who assisted at the funeral service[101] of the woman for whom she had unwittingly performed her first piece of social service as a babe in arms more than 40 years earlier. (See Chapter 11)

Of Stead, Florence wrote: 'Mr Stead, I think, thoroughly enjoyed his incarceration.' Small wonder! Following three days as a common convict in the ominously named Coldbath-in-the-Fields, he was transferred at the bidding of the Home Secretary to Holloway, where, as a 'misdemeanant of the first division,' he was shown every kindness. 'My stay in Holloway ... was a period of

From top left: Catherine Booth, 'The Army Mother'; Catherine (Bramwell-) Booth as a cadet in 1903; Bramwell with his father, General William Booth, Founder of The Salvation Army; Florence in retirement

From top left: Florence as leader of the Rescue Work; Florence with Adelaide Cox, her successor as leader of the Women's Social Work; 'Funny man, all toes!' said two-year-old Catherine, in 1885, of Frederick de Latour Tucker, Army pioneer to India; in the schoolroom – left to right: Catherine, Miriam, Bernard, Florence, Olive and Mary

From top left: Florence with her second child, Mary; Florence as leader of the Rescue Work; Elizabeth Sapsworth with ear trumpet; Katie Booth, 'la Maréchale', on her departure for France in 1881

From top left: W. T. Stead in prison uniform; the young Florence Soper as a new Salvationist in 1881; in the schoolroom (left to right) Miriam, Catherine and Mary

unbroken joy,' he wrote. 'Never had I a pleasanter holiday, a more charming season of repose.'[98] Admitted Florence, 'I almost came to feel that it might have been better if my dear one had had to yield to compulsory rest of that kind, instead of being immersed in the overwhelming strain of Salvation Army work immediately.'[95] Stead's life came to a dramatic – some would say tragic – end with the sinking of the SS *Titanic* in 1912. Bramwell's earthly life would come to a tragic – some would say dramatic – end in 1929, the result of having been immersed in the overwhelming strain of Salvation Army work for close on 60 years.

It will be remembered that Rebecca and Stead had been found guilty of abducting the child without her *father's* consent. Ten years later it transpired that Armstrong was not Eliza's father at all; she was, in fact, the illegitimate daughter of Mrs Armstrong.[99] Had this been known at the time of the trial, the case, of course, would have collapsed.

And what of the wounds the Army had expected to sustain? 'The trial did the Army a great deal of good,' declared Bramwell. 'It made us known, and put us at one stroke in the very front rank of those who were contending for the better treatment of the lost and the poor; and while it roused some powerful enemies, especially in the Press, the enmity lasted only for a time, while the sympathy which was generated remained and remains a permanent possession. Our work for women was greatly furthered by these strange circumstances. We gained friends in political circles, won recognition from the Government then existing and from its successors, and were brought into touch with Queen Victoria and with some of her Court who ever since have been interested in what we have been doing. We knew ... that the Queen followed the proceedings with great concern and sympathy. The case opened doors for us also in the oversea Dominions, and in the United States, and the sympathy materialized in financial help, which, if not at the time large in amount, was encouraging in character.'[100]

In spite of the fact that the rescue work brought its 24-year-old leader great anxiety, often leaving her overtired and overburdened, the publicity afforded by the Maiden Tribute affair resulted in its rapid growth. The staff of four in 1885 numbered 40 by March 1888 and 70 in a further three months. As the Founder pointed out at the fourth anniversary of the rescue work, 'That band of women came from various classes – some, like the ordinary workers in The Salvation Army, from the very class we are endeavouring to save. This is a peculiarity of the Movement ... we turn the saved into the saviours of the class to which they formerly belonged. Others are motherly matrons, who lavish their affection on these poor girls, and others come from higher ranks in life, having abandoned homes of luxury and refinement and devoted themselves entirely to the work.' Ten homes accommodating a total of 212 women and girls were by this time spread throughout the British Isles, 'and on average', claimed the General, 'we could save a girl for seven pounds'.[102]

Since September 1885 *The War Cry* had regularly carried 'An offer of help in seven languages', in which it invited 'parents, relations and friends in any part of the world interested in any woman or girl who is known or feared to be living in immorality, or in danger of coming under the control of immoral persons, to write stating full particulars ... and if possible a photograph of the person in whom the interest is taken. All letters, whether from these persons, or *from such women and girls themselves*, will be regarded as strictly confidential. They may be written in any language, and should be addressed to Mrs Bramwell Booth.' Even before this invitation had gone out, hardly a day went by without Mrs Bramwell's diary recording yet another list of names of those to whom she had written. By the beginning of February 1886 signs of exasperation were showing: 'Wrote letters all the time till starting for Officers meeting. This letter-writing is becoming a great question.'

By the time the first issue of *The Deliverer* (a monthly magazine featuring Salvation Army rescue work) appeared in July 1889, 2,099 women and girls had passed through the homes, of whom 1,676 had proved satisfactory. That year the Founder was reported to have remarked that 'as a rule we took the very worst, and he was not sure but, as a rule, we succeeded best with the very worst'.[103]

Two years later his daughter-in-law went on record as saying she considered that 'one of the first duties of a rescue officer is to take a stand firmly against the position that women guilty of immorality are *worse* than other transgressors. The Salvation Army has nothing but scorn for that code of morals which welcomes a repentant adulterer – if he happens to wear broadcloth – into the drawing room, and introduces him to the daughters of the house, while considering it the height of condescension to admit a repentant sinner of the other sex to be a kitchenmaid in the scullery.

'We believe absolutely in the salvability of every soul. The girl who enters the door of an Army home comes from a world where nobody, as far as she can see, believes in anybody else's goodness. She knows nobody to believe in, and she believes in herself least of all. The atmosphere which she breathes from the moment she crosses our threshold is full of that sort of faith in God which involves high faith in the possibilities of every human creature he has made. Heretofore, from the time of her first fall, she has been expected to be bad. Now, she is expected to be good; and, as a rule, she *is* good. Considering the shattered nerves, the habits of drinking, the craving for excitement, the restlessness of mind and body with which a woman who has been for any length of time leading a sinful life comes to our homes, we could sometimes wonder ourselves as pronouncedly as do others at the large percentage who have been permanently reclaimed therein.'[104]

But not all rescue girls were relegated to being kitchenmaids in the sculleries of the condescending, in spite of the fact that a servants registry had become a going concern by the end of 1887.[115]

'Every fresh trade which looks at all feasible is hailed by the rescue officers as likely to employ fingers and brains which have failed to be useful elsewhere. Bookbinding is proving one of the best,' workshops having been set up to employ a score or more girls.[116] Then there was the thread of yellow yarn – stretching from Mrs Cottrill's 1884 red jersey cross-stitchers, through the needles of the 1885 Salvationist Old Bailey knitters, to the knitting-machine operatives of 1888.[117] 'Washing texts' (presumably 'washable'), underclothing,[118] shirt finishing,[119] upholstering[120] – the list of employment opportunities is endless – and finally, in 1891, despite Mrs Bramwell's five years of determinedly keeping *off* the laundry work, a laundry was taken over.[121]

As early as 5 February 1885 Florence had recorded in her diary the fact that as a result of the 'little talk' she had with them on the subject, two of her rescue girls wanted to emigrate. 'It will be well if they can,' she commented, and in all likelihood they did, for *The War Cry* had already carried the announcement that 'Mrs Bramwell Booth would be very glad to get any information as to how she can assist those of the rescue girls who wish to emigrate, to do so'.[105] Evidently the requested information was quickly forthcoming for in April *All the World* reported Hanbury Street refuge 'jubilant ... over a letter from the very first girl who ever came into the refuge. After having earned a good character in a situation, she was, by the kindness of some friends in Whitechapel, enabled to emigrate, and writes from her situation in Canada.' That emigration was a subject surrounded by fears at this time comes over clearly: 'She says she realised when crossing the ocean that "the past was under the blood", and that, if the ship went down, Heaven's gates were open for her.' It was to be another six years before the Army's own emigration department came into being as part of the Founder's Darkest England Scheme.

Among the original six girls received into the refuge in May 1884 was one so fondly attached to her baby that she dreaded being separated from it. During the first little meeting held in the kitchen she found the Saviour and began to give steady proof of a real change of heart. Work was procured for her at a laundry (this obviously pre-dated Florence's decision to keep *off* the laundry work) and a few things provided to furnish a room, the baby being kept at a neighbouring crèche during the day. But since the young mother seemed incapable of graduating to ironing, she was only able to earn eight shillings a week, and to do that stood at the wash-tub 12 hours a day.[106]

Inevitably her health broke down and the rescue officers had to find lighter work for her, as well as assisting with rent and the support of her baby.[107] This proved to be their earliest involvement with that Victorian euphemism known as 'the double difficulty'. By the time the Army's organisational powers caught up with its rapidly expanding rescue work four years later, and produced commissions for the first already-on-the-job rescue officers, the 'double difficulty' off-shoot had become an integral part of that work, with the first of a string of mother and baby homes being established in Chelsea early in 1886.[108]

By October, Salvationist midwife Mrs Carrie Frost was in charge of the home. With other officers she nightly patrolled such districts as Charing Cross till the early hours of the morning in search of girls in distress. The first pregnant girl was sent to the home at the end of November, her confinement taking place there on 24 February 1887.[109]

As early as June of that year there was talk of the possibility of a small maternity hospital being opened under the auspices of the rescue work.[110] Although dear to the heart of the doctor's daughter from Blaina, it was to be another seven years before this materialised.[111] Meanwhile, other advances were transpiring on the medical front. In September 1891 Florence revealed to readers of *The Deliverer*: 'One small department of our work in which we have met with much success has, I think, been scarcely mentioned in these pages, and I am anxious that friends should understand that we have now a competent band of trained nurses in connection with our maternity home, whom we would gladly send to any part of the country. ... Hitherto ... we have had most numerous testimonies from their employers, speaking both of the efficiency with which their duty has been performed, and of the comfort and happiness they have brought into the household. ... Any young woman who would like to be trained to fill this capacity

123

should apply to me at once, as we are making arrangements for a large increase of this branch of the work.'

This appeal, we are informed in the following issue, was well responded to, and by the Christmas number there are tidings that 'Mrs Bramwell has recently added a small nurses' home, and training operations are now being set on foot, not only for the nurses we need for our own cases, but for many hundreds of friends and [Salvationists] outside. ...'

The August 1892 issue of *The Deliverer* announced: 'Mrs Bramwell is happy in being able to secure the services of an efficient lady doctor for the rescue homes. This, as our readers know, has long been Mrs Bramwell's earnest wish. Our dear friend, Doctor Wilson, who has hitherto acted in this capacity, and for whose kind services we have been most grateful, has consented still to act as consulting surgeon. Mrs Bramwell feels that many ladies in the neighbourhood may, like herself, be glad of the services of a medical Christian lady. She is glad of this opportunity of furnishing them with her address. ...'

By May 1894 Florence is writing in *The Deliverer* of the proposed transformation of Ivy House maternity home at 271 Mare Street, Hackney, into a hospital. 'My friend, Major Sapsworth, is taking up this cause for me, and will act as superintendent to the hospital when it is opened' – clear testimony to the observation made by the 24-year-old in her diary entry of 1 April 1886, regarding the far from youthful Miss Sapsworth: 'She is queer, but she improves. ...'

Fifty years later *The Deliverer* revealed what happened next to the 'improving' Major: 'Not to be at an entire disadvantage herself as the future superintendent, the remarkably fresh-minded Elizabeth Sapsworth, now in later middle life, had begun taking a course of lectures in midwifery – through her ear trumpet! She eventually passed all the theory examinations. ...'[112]

This 1894 development of the maternity home into a fully-fledged maternity hospital left Carrie Frost free to pursue fresh paths in the cause of the East End's ever-expanding population.

'Eighteen months ago', ran an 1896 *War Cry* report, 'Mrs Bramwell Booth appointed Ensign Mrs Frost to inaugurate a scheme, which was first called "The Slum Maternity Work". During the short time since then the work has so prospered and branched out that "District Nursing" is now a more appropriate name than the original one.'[113]

'Of the lives they save there is no record – it is an ordinary matter to them to be called to women sinking under their trial for lack of medical aid, and the necessities of everyday life. The case-books compress stories of human woe and sisterly help into something like the following: "Called at Poverty Row at 2:30 a.m. Woman very exhausted. Baby born. No food but dry bread. Attended to mother and child. Sent milk and eggs. Cleaned room." ...'[114]

A mere dozen years after a potato hurled at her by a Whitechapel costermonger's boy had marked the beginning of her 'career' as a Salvation Army officer, these year-by-year developments initiated by Florence and her helpers, were already forming the strong foundation for what has since grown into more than a century of world-encircling service to womankind.

CHAPTER 15

AND IF HE COULD ONLY MAKE ME CLEVERER

THE year 1885 ended with Florence confiding to her diary: 'Felt Cath and the baby to be so very, very precious. Do trust not to love them too much. Yet God likes me to rejoice in them as gifts from Him I know.' The New Year opened with the resolution: 'Must endeavour to live still more cheaply this year. I hope the new girl will be very careful. I am sorry for many things. Bailey is going, but she is so disagreeable sometimes.' Part of endeavouring to live still more cheaply seems to be that Florence embarked on a great flurry of dressmaking. 5 January: 'Cut out jacket for myself with Miss Asdell. Hope this will not prove penny-wise pound-foolish. It is hard work.' 6 January: 'Home all day dressmaking at the wonderful jacket.' 8 January: 'Put braid on jacket etc. ... Cut out Cath's jacket,' which five days later reveals itself to be 'Cath's uniform jacket' (she is two-and-a-half). 9 January: 'Said goodbye to Bailey. Prayed with her. Am sorry it is so unsatisfactory her going. I know I am not experienced and must deal with servants more wisely, but she has behaved very badly. Hicks housekeeps for us until Monday when Alice Vost comes in.'

Earlier that morning Florence had set out to view a possible property for a hospital or refuge. 'Just as we were to get in the cab both horses fell down. The streets are all frozen up fast, the tramways only navigable.' That evening, 'Called for B at Congress [Hall] and came up with EMB [Emma] and HHB [Herbert], the latter came in to 89 and at nine o'clock we all sat down to dinner.

This is very _bad_. I must persuade him to do better. Conversation about the Trinity and the offices of the Holy Ghost. Also, did Christ descend into Hell?' 11 January: 'Went over the house putting things straight. Very sorry to find Bailey has left things in such a filthy state. ... Kitchen cupboards all had to be turned out – made us very tired. ... Alice Vost arrived about 4. Seemed very pleasant and likely to take an interest in her work. Hicks very useful. B $1^1/_2$ hours late – rather a pity for the first evening.'

Life for the 24-year-old was becoming more and more of a juggling act, and inevitably it took its toll. Saturday 10 July 1886: 'Taken ill Saturday evening. Obliged to lie up. Am very sorry about this because of the weakness and predisposition again it will cause; and grieved and disappointed to lose the expected one.' 12 July: 'Ill. Mrs Heywood Smith called. Thinks I ought to have had the Dr immediately. He might perhaps prevent it. I do not feel so or think it right. Feeling very low and weak. Mrs Railton called and went on to training home to see if either nurses (sic) were free to come. Hudson came.'

13 July: 'Miscarriage came away today. Must believe it is all for the best but feel so very weak and ill and must lie long.' 18 July: 'Impossible to write during these days. Could only lie and think, not even read much or pray.' 20 July: 'Downstairs on couch.' 22 July: despite feeling 'very exhausted and ill' she travelled with the children and Miss Asdell to Brighton.

25 July: 'Felt very poorly. Found the darling children rather tiring and Catherine naughty more than once today. Began over her washing and the cold water with Miss A this morning. I had to get out of bed and go up; and in the evening of singing hymns, would not clap her hands. Sent out the room once, but only back to do the same thing. Obliged to take her out. Spoke quietly to her and smacked her, leaving her alone on the chair. She came in and was quite good till bedtime, singing nicely "Jesus loves me". I feel my inability so much with the children, dearly as I love them; and they both have such strong wills. I earnestly desire to be fitted to train them. God can give me the right power. This specially I claim, even

though unable to do much for them just now. ...Not felt a very profitable day. Have been in darkness for some days in prayer. If the Lord would please to reveal Himself again ... I seek His blessed face.'

Back at home, Florence undertook her first day's work at the refuge on 3 August. The children were not returning for a couple of days. 4 August: 'Home about 4. Find the days much easier when the house is quiet to come to – no darlings to runabout after. It is just the two works combined that are killing me, but it will be better to die than not do them.' By 6 August the children are home and the nursemaid is being unreasonable: 'Felt very poorly and worried. ... Felt very downhearted. Oliphant in to dinner. It is a long time since we were alone in our own house – but this must be for the Kingdom – though how I can make housekeeping ends meet this year I do not know. Cut out my black jacket.'

Left to herself, she could have followed no dearer desire than to be all day long with her two 'treasures'. 'Ministering to the babies, their washing, dressing, and feeding was perfection of happiness. To possess riches is very tempting for the sake of the children. To be able to give them ponies to ride and beautiful grounds to run in, safely sheltered from the dangers of the road, must be a delightful prospect; but to relinquish the joy of caring for them, to miss perhaps the first moment of loving recognition, or the earliest spoken word, would, indeed, have been a deprivation to me. The rich, I think, often lose this joy of service to their little ones.' [122] Yet even in this 'living still more cheaply' juggling act of a household, there were bound to be some 'misses'.

Her diary entry for Sunday 9 October 1887 is a case in point: 'This will I believe prove to have been Cath's spiritual birthday.' Cath's parents were snatching a few brief days at Southborough, where they had spent their honeymoon and where they now celebrated their fifth wedding anniversary. In their absence from home, 'Catherine's surrender to God's claim' came about as 'Miss Asdell applied some words of mine in a letter to the child, and they knelt at the sofa together'.[123] Little Catherine was four years old.

Wrote her mother 50 years later: 'Our children were each dedicated to the service of God in The Salvation Army before they were born. How beautiful to me was the knowledge that whether girl or boy, God's loving purpose concerning them was the same. How can I express the joy we felt as each of our seven, one by one, yielded to the influences of the Holy Spirit and took up the cross of discipleship, with its joy in service. The Lord Jesus became real to them all when quite young, and the gracious work of the Holy Spirit convicted them of their need.'[123]

A 'near miss' came about on 13 November 1887, when her grandfather was due to dedicate little Miriam in the Clapton Congress Hall. 'We started the chicks in three perambulators as we thought in plenty of time, reckoning for eleven. The meeting began at 10.30, so we arrived only just in time. I gave babs a few drops and went in. She was good all the time but fidgety – my arms did ache – she would crow, too. Mama spoke first and at length; when she took baby and laid her down, baby just gave one little cry to sit up.' Although she was only four, the service made a great impression upon Catherine, and on her return she said to her father: 'Mama has given baby right back to God, right back!' But when he looked serious she added, 'Never mind, she's coming home in the perambulator all the same.'[123]

Although Miriam had been born on 18 June, by 2 July: 'No name fixed for baby yet. The General does not like my choice – Salome.' One could be forgiven for supposing that the nearly five-month wait before the dedication was occasioned by arguments over the choice of name. ('Well, we won't *argue* about it, will we?' I can still hear Miriam's nearly 100-year-old sister Catherine declaring when I dared to disagree with her on some matter in the early 1980s.) However, the delay was more likely due to the Founder's demanding itinerary.

During the weeks following Miriam's birth Florence's apprehension regarding her juggling act, never far from the surface, came to the fore. 1 July 1887: 'Am still feeling very weak and have felt very burdened with thoughts of the future. How am

I to do what ought to be done for the rescue work and the three? My only chance is to rise from this bed so filled with God's Spirit that I may have more wisdom how to use my strength for the Kingdom alone. The two chicks have been rather troublesome – dear Cath many times naughty over her reading. Miss Asdell been here all the time – a great help. I do not know what I should have done without her.'

9 July: 'Walked a little today for the first time. Felt sorry almost my little quiet time is coming to an end. Whenever I think of all the work that has to be done I am almost despairing. It seems as if it would be impossible to get through.' 10 July: 'Praying God will give me strength to do just as much work as He wants and leave the rest in peace. Let me discern how much I should do for the three chicks and how much of outside. And if He could only make me cleverer.'

Constant references in Florence's diaries to Miss Asdell require that we identify her. Marianne Asdell (Zazie as the Booth children called her) was a pretty young woman of 25 who had come to help as an officer in the early days of the rescue work. As the diaries show, she often assisted Florence with the children, and for many years lived in their home, going to and from her Salvation Army appointment.[124] In 1902 she was placed in charge of The Nest, the Army's first home for little girls.[125] Six months before Florence had confided 'I do not know what I should have done without her', she had declared: 'Miss Asdell is very trying sometimes in manner and in some narrownesses but it is good for me. It would be very bad to have always congenial people around.'

Of another sometimes trying relationship she was able to write with hindsight: 'My association with the Army Mother during the first eight years of married life was of untold help. She warned me so earnestly against allowing disobedience when the children were young, that I consider my effort to carry out her advice contributed largely to our success in training them. They were all strong-willed as healthy intelligent children should be, and but for my desire to please Mrs Booth it would have been easy to let them get the upper

131

hand. The struggle for the mastery with each one came upon me unexpectedly. In reading my diaries it has been interesting to note the various occasions recorded.

'The tussle with little Mary took place at nineteen months old. On 29 November 1886, I wrote: "Long battle this afternoon with darling baby. There have been threatenings of a storm for a few days, as she has been refusing to kiss people. Would not even kiss me on Friday for a new dolly, so I did not let her have it. Today I went in with some grapes. She had just come in from her walk, so good and bright, but she would not kiss me, and I was with her two and a half hours before she yielded."

'Not one of them was ever punished in haste. When a battle seemed inevitable, I arranged the circumstances to make surrender easy. As few commandments as possible, but no transgression excused from penalty, was the law of the nursery. ...

'There was no margin to the Chief's salary which could provide governesses or tutors, and we were anxious to keep them at home. I was able to be with them from nine to eleven-thirty in the morning and gave the rest of the day to the rescue work, taking the babies to the office so long as I was necessary to their well-being. ... Catherine's influence secured discipline in the schoolroom during "preparation hours" in my absence. Playing with the clay in the garden developed a taste for modelling, and before Mary left home for Salvation Army service she succeeded in executing a bust of her grandfather, a replica of which is to be found in many homes today.'[126]

On 6 January 1886, *The War Cry* announced that the Army Mother was gravely ill. Over the next four years she fought a long and courageous battle with cancer – repercussions of which sometimes cast shadows on her relationship with her Soper daughter-in-law, as on 12 October 1886: 'Went over to see Mama in the evening as I had not been satisfied since a talk on Monday. She seemed to have thought I misrepresented her. Hope we have set things right. This is very grievous to me and a great burden, but I can rejoice before God. He knows my heart is <u>perfect</u> towards

Him and the Army and He will bring it all out right in the end I am sure. Mama is much tried.'

On 4 October 1890 Catherine Booth was promoted to Glory. 'The coffin with a glass lid was taken to the Congress Hall, Clapton, where thousands of people passed by to look on her face. The manifestations of love and reverence were remarkable, many kneeling to consecrate themselves afresh to God's service. Before the public were admitted, on October 8, I took Catherine and Mary and lifted them up to look upon the dear face once more. We talked about Heaven and meeting Grandmamma again and little Mary, five years, seemed greatly distressed – lacking assurance that she really belonged to Jesus. We knelt together and the miracle happened. How happy I am that in some similar way the definite knowledge of their own surrender of will and the smile of Jesus came to them each.[123]

'Love is an able teacher, but as I read the brief records I wish I had been trained to be a mother. I feel I should have done so much better for the eldest had I had some teaching and experience. I fear I was sometimes too exacting.

'I have smiled over some entries written at the time in all seriousness. It was partly because of Mrs Booth's very high ideals that I became too anxious. Perhaps she had forgotten a little of her own actual experience. Once when she was dissatisfied with the behaviour of the babies (they were not more [than babies] while she lived), she said of the youngest: "Baby ought not to dare ask for a thing twice." A few days after this conversation I write: "Dear chicks went up to see the General in the evening. He is alone. Came back romping with Tommy D (the son of the housekeeper). Had to be sent to bed in disgrace. I wish I could see more backbone in precious Cath on these occasions. She is perfectly obedient, but not able to bear any responsibility alone." She was six years old the month before!

'On a later birthday, 1894, our gift was a bicycle made for her by Mr Stanley (the Rover Cycle Co) who was a friend of our work. Diary entry: "The dear child was very delighted with her cycle and

133

went out to ride on it. How my heart yearns over her. She is richly endowed in many ways but needs more grace. In our life of rush and worry I hardly know how to foster in them the love of prayer and of communion with God as I should wish."

'After more experience I learned not to be impatient, and wrote to my husband about one of our boys: "I think it best not to take him to too many meetings. We must avoid spiritual indigestion."'[127] Which of the boys would that be – Bernard, born in October 1889, or Wycliffe, the last of the tribe, after whose birth she was so gravely ill? There were two more girls between the boys, and their mother wrote in later life: 'My cup of happiness in motherhood was filled during the next few years, Olive coming to us in Aug 1891, Dora in 1893, and Wycliffe on Dec 7, 1895. What a very happy party they were! At Hadley Wood [to where they had moved by this time] I was able to let them run about without shoes and stockings, a great saving of my mending time and also of money, with gaiters to keep the legs warm in winter. I found the friction on the hard ground kept their feet beautifully warm. I often wished the poorer mothers in the cities could have done the same. …The gift of a small governess cart gave them great pleasure. How delighted Bernard was to take his place as the pony between the shafts that I might drive to the station or be brought home in triumph when I returned in the evening.[128]

'I reaped the advantage of the good education my father had given me, as it enabled me to teach the children myself.[126] I did not bring them into the schoolroom until they were seven years old, but our third girl, Miriam, taught herself to read in play; she was very bright, and followed the songs and the Bible readings at home and in the meetings. I took them all three to a large gathering in the Crystal Palace, where there was a Solemn Assembly in the Central Transept. Orchestra and nave were crowded and everyone was supplied with a programme; the children sat at the side of the orchestra with an attendant, and when the time of silent prayer at the close of the meeting came, having read the instructions on the programme inviting anyone who would give their heart to Jesus to rise and kneel at the front, little Miriam came climbing down the steps. Her grandfather saw her, and thought she was coming to me at an awkward moment, but finding her sobbing, with the words, "I want Jesus to forgive me," he let her kneel at his chair and later beckoned to me to speak to her.[123]

'My husband and I were satisfied that we were rightly guided in not sending our children away from home. Some advantages they undoubtedly lost, but essentials were not sacrificed. ... A note in my diary in April 1896 runs: "Pleasant walk in the morning with B; talked over plans for the future; arranged our furlough. ... Spoke of the children's education. He helped me to see that it was better to keep Catherine (13 years old) away even from classes (which she might have joined at the girls' school a few doors away). The influence of competition is not good. That a child should be led to think any better of herself because she does better than another or worse because she does not do so well, is not helpful. So for the present I go on doing the best I can!"[127]

'After our dear Catherine, my right-hand helper at home, had left in 1903 to become an officer, the early years of the [twentieth] century found me heavily burdened with work and responsibility. In my position as leader, though I was ably seconded by Commissioner Adelaide Cox [fellow sandwich-board carrier during the French expedition] and Mrs Colonel Barker, I was still needed at the Women's Social Headquarters' office table for some hours during the week, and meetings with different groups of the women, with officers in council and with public gatherings in order to make the work known, absorbed my time. In addition to these gatherings in connection with the rescue work, I frequently went at the weekend for public meetings, and for several years I held a series of weekly Holiness Meetings in the spring and autumn in London.

'The claims of home and these outside calls needed some fitting in. When not away for the weekend I planned to be in the schoolroom by nine o'clock, after family prayers, and instructions in the kitchen as to the arrangements for the day, but as Sunday meetings in the provinces were fairly frequent the timetable on Monday was an alternative one, and the more serious class-work was left for the four mid-week days. I usually left for the office by the 12.46 train, and two and a half hours spent in the schoolroom were very pleasant indeed to me. Catherine had taken the keenest interest in her lessons and succeeded in inspiring her sisters with the same spirit. ... So far as actual instruction went, I had been her sole teacher.'

When editing a collection of Catherine's poetry for publication as she approached her hundredth birthday, I deduced that her 'sole teacher' must have been somewhat weak on punctuation – as attempts at deciphering the diaries have confirmed. But then, had not she, in turn, been educated by her aunts Levick?

'At any rate,' continued Florence (she would have pronounced it 'tanyrate' as her daughters always did), 'I enjoyed my teaching, in spite of the conflict with my many other claims. Is there anything more entrancing, when pupils are eager to learn? On looking through my diaries at this time I am astonished myself to see how very occupied I was, and wonder how I got through it all. I am not surprised that the words "very tired" are frequently to be found in their pages.

'In later years the claims at home became more urgent, and, to my regret, I found it impossible to give the children adequate attention in the schoolroom. Mary and Miriam were able to go to a nearby school for some classes, and I found assistance from visiting teachers for the four younger ones, Bernard, Olive, Dora and Wycliffe, a small legacy from a great-aunt helping with the expense.[129]

'No promises have appeared to me so great and so precious as the promises of God for our children. ... It has been an inexpressible joy to give my one life to Salvation Army warfare; but it is a still greater joy to see the children growing up, preparing to take their places in the ranks, and to uphold and carry forward the work begun by their grandparents, and which is more than life to father and mother alike.[124]

136

'The children all served their soldiership at the Barnet Corps. Before the advent of bicycles this involved a very long walk for small children. I know our neighbours when we first came to live at Hadley Wood were much amused as the party sallied forth from 55 The Crescent East – Catherine, Mary, and Miriam, three small children wearing the poke bonnet. Later, a suitable hat carrying the Salvation Army ribbon band was arranged for junior soldiers, so that our daughters did not wear the bonnet again until they were enrolled as senior soldiers and had signed the Articles of War.'[123] Attendance at the corps involved going to three meetings on a Sunday, the little ones taking great delight in selling *The War Cry*.[128]

One by one the older children became engrossed in Salvation Army activities further afield. 'These were often not helpful to their studies in the schoolroom, however, as they involved postponing the bedtime hour, as for example when Mary and Miriam went to the largest of the Shelters [for the homeless]. How gaunt and despairing those derelict men appeared! Our darlings sang sweetly and talked to them and themselves distributed bread to the eight hundred hungry men. They told me the next morning that they dreamed all night of the hands outstretched. Such opportunities gradually drew them out in love for the poor and sinful, but I sometimes wonder whether they should have been subjected so early to such great emotional strain.'[129]

Embarking on her officer training in May 1903, the third Catherine Booth's first letter home to 'My own darlings' revealed '… the exam is all over. I could not remember how to spell "heaven" so you can all guess my feelings …'[123] Her mother would have understood – she who had confided to her diary on 18 July 1887: 'Glorious day at the Alexandra Palace. No time to write description. Went through agonies at my rescue meeting with nervousness – a terrible echo that sent back all your words. I made a very poor speech.'

CHAPTER 16

FOR WANT OF A BETTER NAME

ONE of their few and far between holidays took Florence and the three little girls to Barmouth at the beginning of August 1887, where they were joined by Dr Soper. It was a perplexing time for her, missing Bramwell so sorely and finding that 'dear Papa seems no nearer being right with God'. Her diary for 21 August continues: 'Dear Lil [sister] and Didz [aunt] have a very miserable time at home. The first few days at Barmouth he seemed in quite a temper all the time, but brightened up afterwards. He is so kind and loving sometimes. It all might be so happy if he would only yield.' A year or two later: 'When, with four of our children, I spent a Christmas at home, the chief joy ... was my father's happiness in me and his delight in our three little girls. The Blaina Salvation Army band came, forming a large ring on the lawn. The display of their uniforms and shining instruments amply compensated for the first Christmas when I belonged to the smallest and poorest group of carollers.'[12]

Her brother and sisters participated in the difficulties their father's opposition created. Before she left home for Paris back in 1881 she had shared her newfound joy with them and they knelt with her to give themselves to Christ. 'My brother felt that he could not add to his father's sorrow by joining The Salvation Army, and when at Oxford, after taking his degree, entered Wycliffe Hall as a preparation for the ministry of the Church of England. He is naturally somewhat shy and retiring, but his love for The Salvation Army brought him to his feet to champion our cause upon one occasion in a debate at the Oxford Union Society.

139

When my brother was a curate at St James' Bermondsey ... his intercourse with us and the influences of the meetings he attended renewed his sense of call to The Salvation Army, and he was accepted as a candidate and entered the training college in 1900.

'My sisters were among the first women to use the bicycle, but unfortunately the hills of Wales, the heavy machines and cumbrous clothing from which women of those days were not emancipated, proved too much for the strength of my younger sister, Evelyn, when they were caught in a storm of wind and heavy rain some distance from home. She suffered afterwards from valvular heart trouble and could only undertake the lighter duties of Salvation Army service.

'My elder sister [Lilian] gave herself whole-heartedly to the Women's Social Work in Plymouth. ... Forty years ago [in the mid-1890s] she began to visit the police courts and the women's side of the prison. ... Colonel Barker ... secured the consent of the prison commissioners for The Salvation Army to conduct a service in the prison. The governor of the prison, the chaplain, and the chief constable were warm friends of our work.

'My sister wrote to me: "On Sunday morning we were at the prison. The men and women were seated before us in crescent formation ... a high partition ran down the centre, dividing the men from the women. The chaplain read the service and then explained our presence and called upon Colonel Barker to speak, and then upon me. We spoke from the pulpit. The governor announced that any prisoner who wished to speak with us (the men with the colonel, the women with me) were at liberty, on leaving the chapel, to take off their number badge and leave it on the book rest in front of them. I cannot tell you what happened with regard to the men, but of the women all but one did so, and I visited them later in their cells." I suppose my sister has the distinction of being the first woman to speak from a Church of England pulpit, and there was a curious sequel, for some time afterwards we heard that the prison commissioners were angry, having had no idea that their consent for Colonel Barker and Captain Soper to do this had included a woman. ✎

'My diary for Sunday 25 February 1906 reads: Meetings in Belfast, taking Mary [now almost 21] with me. ... We were in the Ulster Hall in the afternoon. ... My brother – who was in Belfast, second-in-command at one of the corps, played the organ, and Mary her violin.'[128]

Long before 1907 dawns, the diaries are being written in another hand and are no longer therefore so intimate. Nevertheless, secretary or no secretary, there are still significant happenings to be recorded. January 10, 1907: 'Came up by 2.41 [train] to IHQ for preliminary "Home League" meeting.' January 24: '... Saw Mrs Higgins re Home League ...' February 5: '... Saw Brigadier Sowden re Home League ...' The result of these three meetings was headlined in *The War Cry* of 9 February as an 'Important New Departure'. Mrs Bramwell was reported as having 'undertaken a new, interesting, and, it will be freely admitted, a difficult and yet needful crusade. It is nothing less than an attempt to help mothers by advice, sympathy, and friendship, in the management of their homes. ... Mrs Booth is fortunate in possessing several valuable allies for ensuring that the departure will have at least a fair chance of succeeding. The time is certainly opportune for an experiment in this direction. On all hands it is agreed that the proper place for the application of the laws of hygiene, system, and the principles of thrift is the home. But how are homes to be reached and the parents assisted in a way that will not suggest undue interference?

'It will be conceded, we believe, that the Army (to say nothing of the departments grouped under the direction of Mrs Booth) is in a better position for undertaking work of this description than it was. It has the confidence of the masses. The uniform is practically a guarantee of disinterestedness, earnest endeavour, common sense, and Christian love. It has officers of practical experience. Last, but by no means least, Mrs Booth has the necessary enthusiasm, tact, and persistence for overcoming the initial prejudices and difficulties that are certain to be encountered.'

In her 'Personal Notes' in *The Deliverer* of March 1907, Florence herself described this new departure: 'Very quietly and unostentatiously, a new department has been inaugurated in Salvation Army work and methods. The General has authorized the formation of what we propose to call – for want of a better name – The Home League.' Formally launching the League, she pointed out to the gathering of 'Officers' wives' that 'England was deteriorating because the standard of home-life was being lowered. The flocks of young people in the streets and in music-halls and other places of entertainment were symptoms of this deterioration. One of the main objects of the League would be to combat this tendency, and officers and members of the League would be expected to go about telling people how important home life is. They must begin with the young married people. In many cases the young wife does not even understand the sort of welcome to give her husband when he comes home, hence he slips out to the public house, and that is often the first step to life-long misery. Others do not know the elementary principles of economy, cooking, and general house-management. The League would step in with discretion and sanctified diplomacy, and create an ambition to master these principles.'[130]

On Monday afternoon 11 February 1907 the first local branch of the Home League was formed at Tottenham Citadel 'under most auspicious circumstances', reported *The War Cry* of 23 February. 'Over one hundred wives and mothers listened to Mrs Booth's fascinating address, and it is not too much to say that every one present received a new revelation of the honour, dignity, and responsibilities of motherhood. The practical information on the subject of household management, which Mrs Booth incorporated in her address, was also of the most novel and interesting character, and must certainly have suggested new and better methods to many present.

'Mrs Booth emphasised the practical nature of the Home League by mentioning the fact that it was intended to glean hints for home management, not only from the best authorities in Great Britain, but also from comrades in other lands.

'In this connexion Mrs Booth said that in her own home the French method of cooking vegetables, which is vastly superior to the English way, had been adopted. In another country "hay boxes" had been invented, which would cook food without fuel. It was hoped that these and other useful ideas would be passed on to members of the Home League.

'It would, said Mrs Booth, also be the endeavour of the Secretaries [of the local branches] to so acquaint themselves with all matters pertaining to hygiene that they would be able to render assistance and advice which would considerably reduce doctor's bills. The methods they would adopt would be the same as those practised by a great doctor, who when he lay dying was asked by other members of the profession wherein lay the secret of his success. "I attribute it to all three great physicians," he replied – "Pure Air, Pure Water, and Plenty of Exercise." At the close of the meeting a ready sale was found for a sixpenny work on hygiene, which is now obtainable by Home League members for one penny.'

No doubt already confronted by the patronising attitudes that would stalk it through the years, Mrs Colonel Catherine Higgins, the Home League's first General Secretary, pointed out that it was in no sense a 'mothers meeting', but a 'help one another society'.[131]

Though Mrs Bramwell herself was less than enthusiastic about its name, a century later that same name would be upholding the same aims in all 111 countries of the Army world, its fourfold programme – Worship, Education, Fellowship and Service. By its 50th anniversary the Home League internationally numbered more than 277,000 members.

In the closing decades of the 20th century changing socio-economic factors triggered significant developments in the Army's women's programme. Instead of a simple Home League membership figure, the 2007 *Year Book* gives a Women's Ministries membership of 505,856 (all groups). To unpack that parenthetical 'all groups' would be to discover 'thinking outside the box'

Kingdom-building at its most creative, and although this centenarian 'help one another society' in some long-established territories sometimes looks to be limping behind its progeny, the developing world's home leagues continue to be at the cutting edge of community ministry.

Meanwhile, back in 1907 'the celebration of our Silver Wedding made the autumn very bright for us,' remembered Florence. 'We were at the Homestead [their Hadley Wood home] upon the actual day, Saturday October 12. ... How very happy I was in the unity of both sides of the family. ... I feel that the seal of my own union with The Salvation Army was the fact that my two sisters and brother also gave themselves to serve in its ranks.'

Towards the end of the year 'my father's illness increased and my husband permitted my [officer] brother to be with him. This was a great comfort to us all, as my sisters were away from home. On December 20, 1907, urgent news from Plymouth reached me and I left, but did not arrive until our dear one was unconscious. My brother and I with others watched until in the early hours of the morning his spirit was released. During the last days his intimate talks with my brother relieved us of all anxiety about his future. He was laid to rest with our mother in the churchyard at Blaina. Hundreds of those who had known him as their "beloved physician" came to pay their tribute of affection. I was not able to go to Blaina, for both my sisters were seriously ill.' (Florence had been recalled from Plymouth on the day of her father's death by Lilian's relapse.) 'In spite of pressure of work my dear one went. He was very touched by the tributes rendered to my father's interest in his patients.'[128]

Twelve months later and it was Bramwell's father's health that was causing concern. 'The General's sight had for some time been impaired by cataract. This was a great deprivation to him as it robbed him of a clear view of the people to whom he spoke; he could no longer see their smiles or their tears or so well gauge the effect of his words. The operation on one eye took place on December 16, 1908 at Rookstone [his Hadley Wood home]. In my diary: "Mr Higgens (the surgeon) arrived by the 1.38. Bramwell was present; nine minutes only occupied, cocaine secured painlessness. The General behaved admirably. Bramwell came away with the doctors and returned to the office. The General shook hands with his nurse before the operation, saying, 'Let us be good friends when we begin. There is no knowing what we shall be when we part.'"' The operation met with success.[128]

Six months later, Florence's diary for June 16, 1909, records: 'Hadley Wood – anxious re C.O.S. Serious nervous breakdown.' She remembered this as being a time of extreme anxiety, 'for my dear one was very overdone and had consented to take a long furlough'.

They were staying at their holiday home, Crapstone, in Southwold, when, on 17 August, they 'received news per telephone, of General's breakdown on Motor Tour'. No pleasant holiday tour for the 80-year-old, this. It was one of a series of rigorous evangelistic motorcades he subjected himself to in the closing decade of his life. On this one, a piece of grit spinning off the road surface pierced the good eye, causing him great pain and necessitating its removal. Bramwell and Florence 'decided to travel up by 7:30 train this a.m. to town. Remained in town.' The Founder was to continue in partial blindness until the final test came in May 1912.[128]

These were years of great strain for Florence. The brief diary entries advise us that Miriam, their third daughter, having followed her elder sisters to the training home in 1910, was 'taken away to nursing home' on 15 May 1911, undergoing her 'first operation' three days later. For nearly seven years she was an invalid, 'a mysterious and heart-rending sorrow' for all who loved her, but especially for her parents.[133] She entered Heaven on 12 December 1917.

Meanwhile, at Hadley Wood on Wednesday 22 May 1912: 'Received news of Mary's illness at Hastings' where she was stationed. The following day, leaving ill at home her daughter Miriam and her younger sister Evelyn, 'Went off post haste, 9.45, to Hastings. Mary developed double pneumonia.' Almost as an afterthought she added: 'The General's operation.' This was a reference to the operation on his one remaining eye. It proved a

145

failure, leaving him completely blind. 'The burden and strain upon my husband was overwhelming. He was with his father when the eye was removed, and again at the operation was the one who had to break the news of the blindness, yet he sustained us all.'[128]

Tucked away amid all this anguish comes news that on 4 June 'HRH [Princess Louise] came for the stone laying at the maternity hospital. All went well. HRH so charming. My talking went better than I feared.'[132] The following year, to the veteran superintendent Elizabeth Sapsworth would fall the honour of hoisting the Army flag over the new building – The Salvation Army Mothers Hospital, Clapton.[134]

At Hastings, hope of Mary's recovery had been given up. 'In response to my news, my husband left his father and came to us. We waited together outside the operating room, resigning our treasure to God Who gave her to us. She survived, and after many days of anxiety we took her home to Hadley Wood on a beautiful summer day, June 13, 1912.'[128]

On 6 August Dr Ranger had his last interview with the old General. 'He was very much moved as he came out of the room. On Saturday 10 August the General signed two important documents, which proved to be his last.'

Tuesday 20 August: 'Visiting parties [to bid the General farewell] all day, a great strain on us, but the individuals were very much moved. ... Death released his spirit at 10:13pm.'

21 August: 'Beloved overwhelmed, and so much that he alone can do. He and I went to IHQ. The ceremony of opening the document was less of an ordeal than we feared. Beloved so pleased to learn that the decision was made in his mother's lifetime, and on this very date, August 21. That seemed so wonderful ...'[132]

In that document William Booth had decreed Bramwell should succeed him as General of the Army, which, with the first Catherine, they had founded together. And the now no longer young Florence would be at his side, sharing the burden with her beloved, as she had always done.

END PIECE

TOWARDS the end of writing this life of the young Florence Booth, I received word from Switzerland of the promotion to Glory of one of her granddaughters, Major Fleur Booth, daughter of Commissioner Wycliffe Booth and his wife Renee Peyron. Fleur went to Heaven on 19 October 2006 – the 121st anniversary of the charging of the grand jury in preparation for the Eliza Armstrong trial. More significantly, it was also the anniversary of that Half Night of Prayer at Clapton Congress Hall when her great-grandfather had declared, 'If we win, we win, and if we lose, we win.'

In the 1960s Fleur revealed to me that, until she became a cadet a decade earlier, she had been kept totally ignorant of the happenings that had rocked the Army world in 1929. Although the relieving of her grandfather, Bramwell Booth, from the responsibilities of generalship on the grounds of ill health, and the accompanying calling of the first High Council, had grievously wounded her grandparents and deeply affected her parents and their siblings, these things had never been discussed 'in front of the children'. Twenty years later I understood why.

The more astute of the journalists I accompanied to interview Fleur's aunt, the celebrity Commissioner Catherine Bramwell-Booth, in the mid-1980s, had done their homework and knew of her family's involvement in the 1929 debacle. She would never allow it to be touched upon, however. On one occasion, tears welling in her eyes at the pain of the 50-years-ago remembrance, Florence and Bramwell's fifth child – dear, loyal, lovely Lieut-Colonel Olive Booth – explained to me: 'Our father made us promise never to talk about it. "You see," he said, "it wouldn't do the Army any good."'

On the strength of that promise and at 'such time as this' I have chosen not to talk about it either, save to record that Florence Booth lived another 28 years after the death of her beloved, being promoted to Glory on 10 June 1957, fittingly, within three days of the conclusion of the Home League Jubilee Congress.

A young student teacher, I was among that great crowd who gave thanks for her life in the Clapton Congress Hall. As I sat behind staunch friend of the Army, newspaperman Hugh Redwood, I was aware of participating in a milestone of Salvation Army history.

Commissioner Catherine led us in singing 'Who'll be the next?' over and over again as the pallbearers patiently waited with the coffin on their shoulders in anticipation of mounting the steep steps out of the hall. I hoped they caught the rest of the line: 'Who'll be the next *to follow Jesus?*'

General Frederick Coutts recorded in Volume 7 of *The History of The Salvation Army*: 'It was profoundly symbolic that, even as her coffin was being carried … along one aisle out of the Clapton Congress Hall, a seeker should be moving purposefully towards the mercy seat along the other. In death, as in life, her dedication was being honoured by its continuing fulfilment.'

She had indeed 'come to the Kingdom for such a time as this …'.

SOURCES

Author and publisher are listed at the first appearance of each book. Thereafter only the title is given.

[1]Florence Booth, *Chapters from My Life Story* (Sunday Circle) 25 March 1933
[2]Catherine Bramwell-Booth, *Bramwell Booth* (Rich & Cowan, 1933) p149
[3]*Ibid*, p464
[4]*Chapters from My Life Story*, 26 October 1935
[5]*Ibid*, 21 January 1933
[6]*Ibid*, 28 January 1933
[7]*Bramwell Booth*, p151
[8]*Ibid*, 4 February 1933
[9]Bramwell Booth, *These Fifty Years* (Cassell & Co Ltd, 1929) p89
[10]*Bramwell Booth*, p150
[11]Gordon Taylor, *Companion to the Songbook* (International Headquarters, 1989) p143
[12]*Chapters from My Life Story*, 11 February 1933
[13]Harold Begbie, *Life of William Booth*, Abridged Edition (Macmillan & Co Ltd, 1926) p295
[14]St John Ervine, *God's Soldier, General William Booth* (William Heinemann, Ltd, 1934) p527
[15]*Chapters from My Life Story*, 18 February 1933
[16]*God's Soldier, General William Booth*, p523
[17]*The War Cry*, 17 February 1881, p1
[18]*Ibid*, 24 February 1881, p4
[19]Catherine Bramwell-Booth, *Catherine Booth, The Story of Her Loves* (Hodder & Stoughton, 1970) p354 footnote
[20]*Ibid*, p353
[21]*These Fifty Years*, p90
[22]*Bramwell Booth*, p57
[23]*God's Soldier, General William Booth*, p530
[24]*Catherine Booth, The Story of Her Loves*, p371
[25]*Chapters from My Life Story*, 25 February 1933

[26]Maud Ballington Booth, *Beneath Two Flags* (Funk & Wagnalls, 1890) p160

[27]*Catherine Booth, The Story of Her Loves*, p356

[28]*Beneath Two Flags*, p161

[29]*These Fifty Years*, p91

[30]*Chapters from My Life Story*, 4 March 1933

[31]*Bramwell Booth*, p156

[32]*These Fifty Years*, p93

[33]*Bramwell Booth*, p157

[34]*Ibid*, p159

[35]*Ibid*, p160

[36]*Ibid*, p162

[37]*Ibid*, p164

[38]*Chapters from My Life Story*, 11 March 1933

[39]Robert Sandall, *The History of The Salvation Army*, Vol II (Thomas Nelson & Sons Ltd, 1950) p214

[40]*The War Cry*, 12 October 1882, p1

[41]*General Orders for Conducting Salvation Army Ceremonies* (SP&S Ltd, 1989)

[42]*God's Soldier, General William Booth*, p578

[43]*Bramwell Booth*, p174

[44]*Catherine Booth, The Story of Her Loves*, p372

[45]Bramwell Booth, *Echoes and Memories* (Hodder & Stoughton Ltd, 1925) p10

[46]*Bramwell Booth*, p178

[47]*International Social Council, 1921, Official Record* (London: International Headquarters) pp124, 119, 130, 131

[48]*The War Cry*, 27 October 1883, p1

[49]*Bramwell Booth*, pp248-251

[50]*Chapters from My Life Story*, 18 March 1933

[51]*The Deliverer*, May 1921, p37

[52]Madge Unsworth, *Maiden Tribute* (SP&S Ltd, 1954) p4

[53]*Ibid*, p8

[54]*Catherine Booth, The Story of Her Loves*, p388

[55]*All the World*, February 1888, p64

[56]*The Deliverer*, November 1928, p86

[57]*The Salvation War 1884*, p146

[58]*Maiden Tribute*, p39

[59]*All the World*, January 1893, p5

[60]*The Deliverer*, July 1904, p2

[61]*The War Cry*, 25 October 1884, p4

[62]*All the World*, February 1885, p27

[63]*The War Cry*, 6 February 1886, p2

[64]*Catherine Booth, The Story of Her Loves*, p389
[65]*Maiden Tribute*, p41
[66]Rebecca Jarrett's unpublished memoirs, International Heritage Centre
[67]Booth family oral tradition, related to the author by Lieut-Colonel Olive Booth, 17 July 1981
[68]*Echoes and Memories*, p118-120
[69]Josephine Butler, *The Salvation Army in Switzerland* (Dyer, London, 1883)
[70]Alison Plowden, *The Case of Eliza Armstrong* (BBC, 1974) p16
[71]*Maiden Tribute*, 27
[72]Charles Terrot, *The Maiden Tribute, A Study of the White Slave Traffic of the Nineteenth Century* (Frederick Muller Ltd, 1959) p139 forward
[73]Roderick Moore, *Josephine Butler: Feminist, Christian and Libertarian* (Libertarian Alliance, 1993) p6
[74]W. T. Stead, *The Truth about the Armstrong Case and The Salvation Army* (Pamphlet)
[75]*God's Soldier, General William Booth*, p647
[76]*Catherine Booth, The Story of Her Loves*, p391
[77]W. T. Stead, *Pall Mall Gazette*, 4 July 1885
[78]*Bramwell Booth*, p179
[79]*The Case of Eliza Armstrong*, p40
[80]*Echoes and Memories*, p126
[81]*God's Soldier, General William Booth*, p647
[82]*Catherine Booth, The Story of Her Loves*, p394
[83]*Ibid*, p395
[84]*Ibid*, p396
[85]*Ibid*, p404
[86]www.en.wikipedia.org
[87]*The Maiden Tribute, A Study of the White Slave Traffic of the Nineteenth Century*, p170
[88]Rebecca Jarrett's unpublished memoirs
[89]*The Case of Eliza Armstrong*, p11
[90]*Echoes and Memories*, p128
[91]*The Case of Eliza Armstrong*, p14
[92]*Bramwell Booth*, p185
[93]*Ibid*, p247
[94]*God's Soldier, General William Booth*, p654
[95]*Chapters from My Life Story*, 1 April 1933
[96]*The Case of Eliza Armstrong*, p132
[97]*Bramwell Booth*, p184
[98]W. T. Stead, *My First Imprisonment* (E. Marlborough & Co, 1886)

[99]*The History of The Salvation Army*, Vol III, p43

[100]*Echoes and Memories*, p131

[101]*The Deliverer*, April 1928, p9

[102]*The War Cry*, 23 June 1888, p8

[103]*Ibid*, 8 June 1889, p5

[104]*A Brief Review of the First Year's Work* (1891) p117

[105]*The War Cry*, 17 January 1885, p3

[106]*The Salvation War* (1884) p145

[107]*All the World*, April 1885, p87

[108]Unpublished Receiving House Statements, Book 1 (1886) p16a

[109]*Ibid*, p139a

[110]*The War Cry*, 26 March 1887, p9

[111]*The Deliverer*, May 1894, p168

[112]*Ibid*, December 1944/January 1945, p147

[113]*The War Cry*, 23 May 1896, p4

[114]*All the World*, May 1897, p216

[115]*The War Cry*, 19 November 1887, p13

[116]*All the World*, February 1888, p64

[117]*The Deliverer*, November 1891, p72

[118]*The War Cry*, 16 February 1889, p7

[119]*Ibid*, 16 March 1889, p4

[120]*The Deliverer*, December 1890, p89

[121]*Ibid*, March 1891, p144

[122]*Chapters from My Life Story*, 2 November 1935

[123]*Ibid*, 21 December 1935

[124]*Ibid*, 8 April 1933

[125]*The Deliverer*, October/November 1944, p139

[126]*Chapters from My Life Story*, 8 April 1933

[127]*Ibid*, 14 December 1935

[128]*Ibid*, 1 February 1936

[129]*Ibid*, 18 January 1936

[130]*The War Cry*, 9 February 1907, p8

[131]*Ibid*, 30 January 1909, p11

[132]*Chapters from My Life Story*, 15 February 1936

[133]*Bramwell Booth*, p252

[134]*Maiden Tribute*, p67

INDEX

154

155